FINDING
THE
NEXT
Super Stock

By Frank A. Cappiello

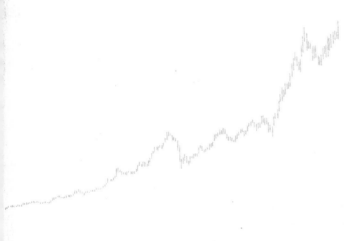

First printing: July, 1982
Second printing: November, 1982
Third printing: February, 1983

© Frank A. Cappiello, 1982

LIBERTY PUBLISHING COMPANY
Cockeysville, Maryland

Published by:
Liberty Publishing Company, Inc.
50 Scott Adam Road
Cockeysville, Maryland 21030

Library of Congress #81-84999
ISBN 0-89709-031-4

The publisher and the author thank the following people for their assistance: Lucien Rhodes for editorial work, and David Blumberg of T. Rowe Price Associates for help with the statistics.

The companies and/or securities listed or featured in this book are examples only and their mention should not in any way be construed as a purchase or sale recommendation.

Manufactured USA

To Marie —
my favorite blue chip

To my friend and colleague —

Of the dozens of panelists who have appeared with me on "Wall $treet Week" since it began in 1970, none has been invited more often or provided more enjoyment and profitable advice than Frank Cappiello.

Those who have kept a long-term score, as I have, know that Frank is one of America's most brilliant securities analysts and guides to investment profitability.

I am delighted (as, indeed, we all should be) that my friend and colleague has now set down, in this book, his own methods for finding "super stocks." He has few peers as a super stock-picker. And, in the better environment for economic growth and equity investing that all rational Americans devoutly hope to see in this decade, we can surely use all the help we can get. Thanks, Frank, for again being there when we needed you, with the substance and the smile.

Louis Rukeyser

Contents

Foreword

Like everybody else, investors make all kinds - and lots of - mistakes. If they didn't, they'd all own the proverbial yachts. During my fifty years of investment counseling, I've looked at thousands of investors' portfolios and have seen at first hand both their successes and their failures.

One of their most common errors is the failure to keep investments in tune with the times — to prune out the dead wood in sick and dying industries — and to put some money into the rapidly growing, successful companies that can offset the inevitable future havoc wreaked by politicians, regulators and tax collectors.

Everybody dreams of finding another I.B.M. or Xerox or Hewlett Packard . . . one of the "Super Stocks," as this volume classifies them. Only a few thousand dollars put into any of these companies as they were rolling down the runway catapulted their lucky owners into the top tax brackets.

And as our author points out, the *best* time to search for potential Super Stocks is in a period of lack-luster economic activity when uncertainty and gloom are the passwords. In other words, in times such as the present.

The author gives much useful, practical information and advice on how to identify a future wonder stock. He lists the characteristics which all of yesterday's big Super Stocks had in common, he illustrates his selection process with specific examples, and he concludes that tomorrow's big winners will embody most, or all, of these same qualities. This is a helpful, thoughtful volume for investors who are serious about achieving superior investment results.

Out of the thousands upon thousands of stocks available for investment today only a tiny fraction of 1% will turn out to be the actual Super Stocks of tomorrow. Moreover, by the very nature of the hazards inherent in companies with extraordinary growth rates, those companies that now fully measure up to our author's stringent standards can be blown away even before their own managements know what's happening.

Given this background, my caveat to readers is: Don't settle on one or two issues as the potential key to your investment Shangri-La. Pick — by the author's qualifications — a dozen or so and hope you'll be smart enough (or lucky enough) to have chosen at least one of what future investment historians will be calling the I.B.M.'s of the 1980's.

David Babson

Introduction

About five years ago, on a flight to Seattle, I was questioned by a fellow passenger on how to make money on Wall Street. "If I could get the kind of inside information that you people get," she said, "I'd make a fortune!"

She, like so many people, views successful investing as simply profiting from tips, rumors, and trading. It's true, anyone can make a quick trading profit once in a while; and some do it frequently. But making *big* money in the stock market is not quite that easy. Real success on Wall Street requires planning, dedication, and hard work, as with any other business. It is easy to be charmed by stories of people like the taxi cab driver in Rochester, New York, who, based on the advice of one of his passengers, put his modest life savings into Xerox stock in 1958 and emerged a millionaire a few years later. That was pure luck, of course.

Finding super stocks—shares that multiply many times over for sound, fundamental reasons—is not an impossible task. It can be done. . .it has been done. . .and it will be done time and time again in the years ahead.

Every successful investment practitioner I've ever met has a philosophy and a method, along with a battle plan to make it all work. And each approach is carried through with discipline and dedication. However, nearly all require a combination of sophisticated financial, accounting and technical knowledge—*and* a constant flow of timely information leading to the right decisions.

The one method that can work for all investors, professionals on Wall Street or "the little guy" on Main Street, is outlined in detail in this book. This approach has succeeded for countless investors. It is not a secret. In fact, its tenets are known by many experienced Wall Streeters. But it is not widely used because it requires dedication, hard work and, most of all, patience. The method stresses fundamentals, as does consistent success at just about anything. Years of trial and error have been distilled into a score card. The answers found on these sheets will be the result of your research and analysis. The score card will guide you, provide some discipline, and hopefully keep you on track in your search for the next super stock.

This is a "how-to" book for the serious investor. Read it carefully, collect and study company material, refer back to the text, and use the score card. Once you get into it, you'll find that research can actually be exciting and fun. And, in the end, finding a super stock will be not only intellectually satisfying, but financially rewarding. I cannot promise that this book will make you rich. But it might.

Frank A. Cappiello
June, 1982

The Outlook:
Never Brighter!

The Right Time to Invest

How can anyone buy stocks with *any* degree of confidence today? The problems seem insurmountable. Will we never be free of this vicious cycle between inflation and recession? Clearly, unemployment is still too high and interest rates are completely unpredictable. And what of the uncertainty in the Middle East? That cannot be ignored. How can *anyone* be optimistic, let alone make money in the stock market with such an environment?

People have a tendency to see the dangers and problems of the present as being peculiar in what historians call "chronocentrism." The feeling that the past was superior in terms of living quality, safety, and investment opportunity is not unique to our time. Every generation in history has felt that the past was better...including our own childhood. We forget our personal fears and anxieties of adolescence—the uncertainty of early maturity. Indeed, any close review of historical periods that seemed to represent idyllic conditions would reveal anxieties and calamities. Consider the England of Robin Hood and Friar Tuck...of Richard the Lion Hearted. This was a period of clear heroes—well-defined villains and a happy peasantry feasting on venison and wine. Hardly! Robin Hood's England was one of banditry, starvation, and capricious rule by a too-often absent king. Others yearn for the age of faith—of monasteries and St. Francis of Assisi. Actually, the age of Faith was an age of filth—a lack of sanitation, poor diets and even poorer medical care and an early death by most. For Americans—the most tranquil period of our history appears to most to be the early 1900's in the Middle West. We recall the wide vistas of Kansas wheat fields, the large families and mother canning the fruit of the family labors...the Land of Oz, Dorothy and the Wizard. A nice fable, but hardly true. Dorothy (of Oz) would have been worked to death (or boredom) in the Kansas of the 1900's. The family worked from dawn to dusk. They ate well in the summer, if they were lucky, but usually went hungry in the winter. Furthermore, chances were high that one of the children would die of diptheria, or tuberculosis or due to a simple operation in a "hospital."

The fact is, today's problems are not new problems. Concerns of inflation, recession, interest rates and international conflict have threatened investors in one way or another, and in varying degrees, since the end of World War II. A few hours reading old newspapers in the local library will quickly lay fears to rest.

But, is it not true that enormous sums of money have been lost in the stock market over the past twenty years? After all, haven't the bear markets of 1961-62, 1973-74 and 1981-82 taught us anything? Surely, there are better investments than stocks!

Indeed, most observers think that stocks in particular and the stock market in general have been poor places to invest over the past two decades. Using the Dow Jones Industrial Average as an example, they note that the Dow average of 30 stocks hit 1,000 in 1966 and has struggled to pass that level ever since. Take your marbles elsewhere, they say, there are better games in town.

Actually, these financial pundits have overlooked, forgotten, or never knew that there are stocks and then there are *super stocks;* there is a stock market and then there is a super stock market. And they barely know each other.

The Dow is only one of several averages, yet, it is the most widely used indicator of stock prices because its history goes back to the end of the last century. As a result, the Dow (including the transportation and utility indices) has an attractive historical base of data for financial reporters and market observers. But the Dow as a reflector of the overall stock market can be misleading due to its nature and large company bias. It obscures the opportunities being realized every year from the more rapidly-growing segments of our economy. Further, from time to time, companies are added or deleted, which create erratic patterns in the Dow. One of the often-quoted cases in point is IBM. In 1939, IBM was removed from the Dow 30 and AT&T was substituted. Ironically, if IBM had stayed in the Dow, the average would have reached a December high of 1017.39 in 1961! Instead, the Dow was at 734.91. (To add further to the irony, it is worth noting that IBM has since been reinstated as a member of this elite group.)

Other stock market averages have done better than the Dow in the past including the next most quoted index: the Standard & Poor's Stock Price Index of 400 industrial stocks and, like the Dow, the S&P also has financial, transportation, and utility indices. The Common Stock Index, a composite of all equity issues listed on the Exchange, has also appreciated more than the Dow in most recent years. Finally, there are the indices of the smaller companies such as the over-the-counter National Quotation Bureau Industrial Average index and the Value Line composite of 1600 stocks that have both reached new highs while the Dow struggled to regain its former record level. Unlike the Dow, these indices more closely reflect the experience of the past decade, demonstrating that the stocks of small- to medium-size companies have done substantially better than larger companies.

Some experts still point out, by using all traditional measures, that stocks cannot compare with investment returns from non-financial assets such as antiques, gems, Chinese ceramics, and, of course, real estate. And, while this is perfectly true, the experts are again comparing apples and oranges. No, in recent years, most stocks can't hold a candle to certain non-financial assets, but super stocks are another story altogether. They can easily match the return on Chippendale chairs or Persian rugs and frequently do better.

Regardless of the time period selected, super stock examples are everywhere. In 1952, a year riddled with the uncertainties of the Korean War, controls, and concern about the course of the post-war economy, the shares in a small tool company called Black & Decker were available for $35. The company had just declared a 3% stock dividend, the first in a long series

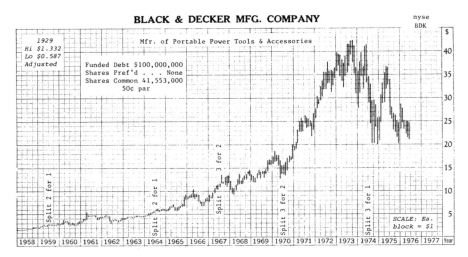

BLACK & DECKER MFG. COMPANY

of stock dividends and splits. By ignoring the problems of the day and analyzing the company's past and potential performance, Black & Decker would have been recognized as a super stock. One hundred shares purchased for $3,500 would have grown to 2,350 shares by late 1973, worth an astounding $286,112 without a single additional dollar of investment in those 21 years. The steadily increasing dividends during that time would have provided thousands of dollars of income.

Between 1968 and 1977, Tropicana Products became a super stock by following a logical idea — squeeze oranges in Florida for Northern breakfast tables rather than pack and ship them with the attendant risk of spoilage. Tropicana backed this idea with an aggressive marketing organization and in ten years expanded its sales from almost $61 million to $246 million. During the same period, earnings per share rose from 22 cents to $2.39. In 1978, the company was acquired by Beatrice Foods. An investor could have purchased Tropicana in 1968 at $4¼ and, adjusted for the Beatrice offer, the profit in 1978 would have been over 1,000%.

In early 1969, the shares of a small specialty chemical producer, National Chemsearch, were listed on the New York Stock Exchange for the first time. Only two years prior,the stock had been quoted over-the-counter at $46 with 1968 earnings projected to be $3.20 per share on sales of nearly $50 million. At the lowest point in the 1974 bear market, NCH stock had suffered a decline of 50% from its high twelve months earlier. Yet, 1968 investors should not have been too concerned. The stock's 1974 low was equivalent to $208 per share, before adjusting for three splits in the meantime. Moreover, by this point in time, the company's sales and earnings were nearly quadruple the levels of 1968. The all-important question then became: Could this growth continue?

In late 1971, Baker Oil Tools, founded nearly 60 years earlier, was enjoying the bounty of success. At $40 per share, its stock, listed on the New York Exchange, had risen 300% from its lows of three years before. For the first time in the company's history, annual sales would reach $100 million and earnings were expected to exceed $1.80 per share! Indeed, prospects seemed bright since this company's products would be used by others wanting to "stimulate" the production of older oil wells. Nine years later, in 1980, Baker's sales rose above $1.5 billion, earnings reached the equivalent of nearly $17 per share on the original stock, and the price of each share, before adjustments for splits, topped the equivalent of $424, a gain of nearly ten-fold.

Of course, today's observer only sees the Tropicanas, the Bakers, and the Black & Deckers in retrospect; after the fact. And even though they are exceptional winners, they are not rarities. In every economic period, whether interest rates are rising or falling, whether the economy ascends or descends, or whether the "cold war" once again heats up, there are winning super stocks. And super stocks will do well even if they are bought at their highs.

Take the year 1966 for example — a time when the inflation rate first began to move up, a war in Vietnam widened, and "Great Society" programs emerged to push inflation even higher. In such an environment, what could be better than the safest of all blue chips, American Telephone & Telegraph? Had AT&T been purchased at its high that year, the results would have been less than satisfactory, however. The high in 1966 was $63. Ten years later, that same stock was again selling for $63. But more "risky" (was it, really?) was Masco, the manufacturer of a basic plumbing item: the Delta faucet. Masco, at the 1966 high, adjusted for splits, was 3¾. In 1976, the stock was 31¾! However, this stock performance did not occur in a vacuum. During this same ten year period, sales rose from $31 million to more than $400 million and earnings per share advanced from 24 cents to $1.80.

The Masco "Delta" kitchen faucet.

By being careful and disciplined about a stock's selection, timing in its purchase will not be a significant factor in the long run. Put another way, the right stock bought at the right time means fantastic price performance. The right stock bought at the wrong time results in substantial price appreciation over time. However, the wrong stock in the wrong market is, and will always be, a disaster!

The best time to invest is right now! Will the "market" be lower a few months from now? Maybe. But this period...and today's prices...will look pretty good to investors five or ten years from now when they look back fondly and say: "Those were the good old days!"

Anthony T. Rossi, founder of Tropicana Products, now part of Beatrice Foods Company.

The Tropicana Train for faster service to customers.

Baker International enjoyed
substantial growth during the
1970's. The company's products
were in great demand and
management made a number of
logical, strategic acquisitions.
Pictured left is the Reed Rock
Bit, one of the leading products
of its kind in the field. Reed
Tool Company was acquired in
1975. Below is Baker's Model
R-3 Casing Packer which is used
to control pressure and seal off
a well's producing zones.

Much of Baker International's success is due to the leadership of E.H. "Hubie" Clark who joined the company as a trainee engineer in 1947 and rose to later become president in 1962. In the twenty years following Mr. Clark's appointment as president, the company's sales advanced from $30 million to more than $2 billion.

Acquisitions played an important role in Baker's progress in the 1970's. By the early 1980's, divisions acquired after 1968 accounted for about two-thirds of total sales and earnings. Two key executives responsible for the company's success in this area were James D. Woods, left, and James Joe Shelton, right.

In 1951 Black & Decker Manufacturing Company sold its one millionth ¼-inch Home
Utility portable electric drill. Shown that year, from left to right, were: Robert D. Black,
Honorary Chairman of the Board; Glen Tressler, Marketing Vice President; Founder Alonzo
G. Decker; Inspectress Nancy Almony; Founder S. Duncan Black, and Alonzo G. Decker, Jr.

Alonzo G. Decker, Jr. joined Black & Decker in 1930, was laid off during the depression,
and was later re-hired as a laborer. He worked his way up to become Chief Executive
Officer in 1964. During the ten years that he held this post, B&D's sales rose from $101
million to $642 million and the company became the dominant factor in its industry.

Unlimited Opportunities

Most Wall Street observers know or have heard the names Joe Wilson (Haloid Xerox), Edwin Land (Polaroid), and William McKnight (3M). These were key executives of what became major corporations during the post-war era. The "movers and shakers," as they are sometimes called, are often in the business news once their accomplishments are better known and their companies become more important.

Indeed, investors who spend time researching young, growing businesses know this to be an on-going, never-ending process of new names and new personalities. And yet many key people still go unnoticed. For example, each of the following men has founded a company that is today a leader in its field: Monty Rifkin, Steven Jobs, Paul Cook, and Frederick Smith...not exactly household names! Monty Rifkin is one of *the* pioneers in the cable television industry and a founder of the country's largest CATV company, American Television & Communications (now a subsidiary of Time, Inc.). Steven Jobs' business, which began in his garage, is Apple Computer, a leading manufacturer of personal computers. Paul Cook founded Raychem Corporation, the leading producer of heat-shrinkable insulation materials for industry. Frederick Smith's report for a college economics course led to the creation of Federal Express, now a leading company in the field of overnight, small-package delivery.

What of the future? Who will be the entrepreneurs and major personalities behind the new business ventures of the late 1980's and 1990's? Only time will tell. However, it is not difficult to identify the areas which hold promise for exciting new growth companies.

A beginning assumption is that private enterprise will endure. Given the proper fiscal and monetary policies, our economic system will continue to have the power to inspire sacrifice, investment, and production. This trend will almost certainly be punctuated by recurring bouts of inflation and disinflation for brief periods, but the overall trend will be up and investors should be constantly alert for new opportunities.

Among the many promising areas in which future super stocks might be found:

Technology
- Business and office equipment.
- Communications, including CATV, satellites, and video and data transmission.
- Computer software.
- Defense electronics.
- Home entertainment and home business systems.
- Materials substitution.
- Micro-computers.
- Robots.
- Specialty chemicals.
- Telecommunications.

Health and Medical
- Drugs and drug administering.
- Health care facilities and services.
- Medical devices.
- Medical equipment and supplies.

Consumer and Business Services
- Business employment services.
- Computer-related services.
- Rental services of all kinds.
- Specialty retailing.

Energy
- Conservation technologies.
- Energy alternatives, including solar and synthetic fuels.
- Extraction equipment.
- Services.
- Transportation using energy-efficient concepts.

Other
- New concepts for manufacturing and production.
- New leisure time products and activities.
- New retailing and marketing methods and services.
- Unique or specialty consumer products for the home or business.

These broad categories are not all-inclusive, of course. They are listed merely to illustrate the many possibilities. As a general rule, the new products and services in the years ahead will offer certain advantages in the marketplace. Most likely, they will be smaller or bigger, faster or slower, more efficient, more attractive, less expensive, easier to use or install, etc., etc. Clearly, the opportunities for new growth businesses are unlimited.

Texas Instruments' development of the silicon transistor in the 1950's led to a revolution in home and business electronics. Shown here is an early model of the transistor radio in 1954, both in its engineering package and as it was sold commercially.

Can You Beat 'Em?

During the 1970's, most professional money managers had great difficulty beating the market averages. This conspicuous lack of superior performance by many of the most skilled professionals on Wall Street inspired some of their clients to ask for an explanation. Since money managers have a certain fondness for steady clients, the explanation was not long in coming. Research that had been done several decades earlier was dusted off and polished up to demonstrate that it was understandably difficult to outperform the market because the market was "efficient." That is, information about public companies is a matter of record, either at the SEC, in newspapers, at the local library, or in some other data source. The sum total of all that information and the judgments based on that information, the efficient market thesis maintained, is at all times fully reflected in the price of any given stock. Since all security analysts have access to every shred of data, they are unlikely to uncover anything new. This felicitous discovery was followed by a second, affectionately described as the "if you can't beat 'em, join 'em" theory. If all a diligent security analyst could hope to do was match the performance of some broad market average, then why not create portfolios predesigned to duplicate the market's results? This was called "indexing" and it means to select stocks that reflect the overall composition of the Standard & Poor's 400 or 500 average. Properly structured, the indexed portfolio would, in fact, be the "market." Not only would it guarantee satisfactory performance, but it would also reduce costs since obviously there would no longer be any need to pay analysts fancy salaries. Things were looking up on Wall Street. They were looking so good in fact that these largely defensive musings were promptly elevated to the emminence of a "theory," known in full as *Modern Portfolio Theory.* Simply stated, it is a theory of securities valuation which attempts to measure investment risk on a scientific basis.

The author of the portfolio manager's kitchen pass was Harry Markowitz, a research scientist who, in the early fifties, divided risk in common stocks into two categories: (1)

market risk (known as "beta"), and (2) non-market risk ("alpha"). He concluded that when the market went down, some stocks performed worse than the market and that when it went up, these stocks did better than the market. A "beta quotient" was assigned to a stock. A beta of 1 assigned to a stock meant that the stock performs equal *with* the market: it would go up and down percentage-wise along with the market. A beta higher than 1 meant it is more volatile than the market and a beta of under 1 meant that it would be less volatile.

Given the power of computers to do the arithmetic and correlations and to sift through enormous amounts of data in short periods of time, it became easy to evaluate all of the better known and better researched stocks in terms of their volatility to the market; i.e., their "betas." From this, it was an easy step to develop portfolios based on "betas." If one wanted a portfolio that would be much more volatile than the market (say, do 20% better in an up market, it was easy enough to select stocks with betas of 1.2 or alternatively put together a package of stocks, some with betas of 1.1 and others with betas of 1.3 or 1.4, so that the average beta of the portfolio would be 1.2). Portfolio management was relegated to simple automation techniques, and the big investors knew the "betas" of all the big stocks. They knew everything there was to know about the IBM's, the DuPonts and several thousands of other large companies whose stocks are heavily traded each day. As one market sage describes it: "It is as if all the institutions are Mach 3 fighter jets — armed with the latest radar to search for targets with their computer-guided missiles. There they are...hundreds upon hundreds of these high-capacity, electronic-powered jets stalking each other, able to assimilate mountains of data in only a few seconds. The jets are much like institutional investors, so evenly matched with their arsenals of high-powered MBA's, that they cancel out each other. When one sells IBM, they all sell IBM. When one buys Standard of Ohio, they all buy Standard of Ohio."

And yet, despite all this sophisticated weaponry and tracking equipment, some investors can and do make money. How come? Because at the same time the market is efficient, it is also inefficient. IBM symbolizes the efficient market. Every analyst on the street and every portfolio manager knows the data of IBM, and it's pretty hard to come up with something new. Every once in a while an analyst will put two bits of information together and get five instead of four—an inspired conclusion that will allow him and his institution to make 10 or 12 points on DuPont or Mobil Oil. But not often. The more widely owned the stock, the more "efficient" the market is in that stock; the more likely that everything known about the stock is reflected in the price.

On the other hand, the smaller the company, the less likely that it has an institutional following and the less efficient the market for its shares is likely to be. Accordingly, with smaller companies, "market inefficiencies" are the rule rather than the exception. . .and it is here where careful analysis can yield a potential super stock.

The professional investors (those who head institutions) make up some 70% of the trading in the stock market. Given their billions of dollars, the emphasis is on buying stocks in companies where a sizeable investment position can be developed without running up the price. In other words, institutions want "size" in their stocks.

According to the SEC, there are 21,000 public companies. Of these, only a fraction, a few thousand, are listed on the various exchanges—the New York and American exchanges, and so on.

Consider, too, that only another several thousand are traded with any degree of volume. The Big Five brokerage houses such as Merrill Lynch, Bache, Dean Witter, etc. each have several dozen analysts assigned to cover several hundred stocks of interest to these institutions. For the most part, these firms each cover the same stocks. Other major research firms cover fewer, although many of these are also duplication coverage in stocks like General Motors, DuPont, etc. Essentially, all of their energies are focused on the large- or medium-sized companies. They have to be. But with all this brainpower focused on those stocks, which constitute the bulk of trading, it's hard for anyone to enjoy an advantage and to have pieces of information unknown to anyone else. Over the years, a number of academic studies have indicated that none of the major players can get an advantage and, for the most part, this is true.

However, while major studies have indicated it is hard to "beat the market" long term, there is also ample evidence that it can be done. Over the years, we in the investment business have observed that certain individuals do beat the market consistently — and when performance statistics are analyzed, it appears that they do it by investing in smaller-sized companies.

Not too long ago, *Fortune* signaled this style of investing in an article entitled: "Giant Payoff from Midget Stocks." (Fortune, June 30, 1980 - A.F. Ehrbar, p. 111-114.) A further study by Professor Rolf W. Banz of the University of Chicago noted that for over 54 years, smaller stocks yielded *twice* the return of stocks listed on the New York Stock Exchange. At this point, a skeptic would say: "But you expect to do better in smaller stocks because you're taking more risk. Higher risk equals high returns, right?" Wrong. Even adjusted for risks, smaller stocks did better.

A little thought will indicate the logic of it all. Again, the big institutions are all zeroing in on the small, but highly-liquid universe of stocks they can buy. Beyond that — no one cares. There are small-size companies in the suburbs of Tucson. . .Seattle. . .Boise. . .even Chicago and New York. . .that the institutions can't buy. And they don't care! At least for the time being. By analyzing these stocks, the average investor is not doing battle with a platoon of MBA's and a bank of computers. Later. . .years later. . .when the junior stock has grown to a sufficient size, it will suddenly be "discovered" and be entered into the thousands of computer banks of institutions and covered assiduously by analysts. At that time, the small, junior stock will soon become a super stock — fully discovered and fully-priced.

The Many Roads
To Success

It is true, there are many roads to success. But on Wall Street, all roads do not necessarily lead to Rome. Not every investment approach is a reliable way to make money over the long term. Yet, there are a few, and they will be described briefly in this chapter.

The methods vary; they can be very different, in fact. The technical analysts track charts and indicators. The "bargain hunters" search the marketplace for undervalued corporate earnings or assets. Many investors look only for "turnaround situations," while "concept chasers" are forever seeking new investment ideas that might catch the imagination of the financial community at some point in the future. And then, of course, there are those who swear by the growth stock theory. (The proponents of this approach believe a stock's value will eventually reflect the company's progress in terms of earnings, dividends and financial condition).

However, investors who pursue these methods are, in their own way, unknowingly, seeking to capture profits from the inefficient segment of the market. They are, in effect, looking for situations not yet fully recognized by the investment community as a whole. Said somewhat differently, to quote the late Benjamin Graham: "There are two requirements for success on Wall Street. One, you have to think correctly; and secondly, you have to think independently."

Indeed, Wall Street history is replete with independent thinkers. In the 1920's and 1930's Bernard Baruch made and lost fortunes by trading on instincts and Joseph Kennedy was known in financial circles for his short selling as the stock market plunged after 1929. But they were traders with a shorter term perspective.

By the same token, there have been many long term investors who may also be called independent thinkers. Certainly, among them, are two famous money managers, David Babson of Boston and T. Rowe Price of Baltimore. In fact, these men are credited for practically inventing the growth stock theory of investing. Both started in the 1930's, in the darkest days of the Great Depression, when no one imagined the possibility of future growth. Both have given their names to large mutual funds and investment management organizations.

Each, with his own style, emphasized taking the long term view. David Babson, for example, would always explain his approach by saying that he wasn't "smart enough" to make money trading in the market. But he felt that the most certain way to achieve positive long term results would be to own shares of successful companies in fields with particularly promising future prospects.This approach to investing, he maintained, would not necessarily give the *best* performance in any given period, but would surely provide better-than-average results over a long span of years. And his record certainly proved him right.

Finally, both expected to pay a premium for growth. They reasoned that if the additional cost was early enough in the game, there would be so much profit in the long run, that a premium could be justified more often than not. So, in retrospect, the most profitable and lowest risk time to buy a stock of this kind was during the early stages of growth. Neither advocated "growth at any cost," but both were pioneers willing to invest for the *future*.

T. Rowe Price

As T. Rowe Price tells it, his investment philosophy on growth evolved back in the 1930's when President Roosevelt took the U.S. off the gold standard. At that point, Rowe Price was convinced that the country would be saddled with continous inflation with only a few interruptions. He felt that investments of bonds or ordinary stocks would not be good enough to offset the lost purchasing power of the dollar. In addition, he recognized the difficulty in identifying and catching the cyclical swings of interest rates and corporate fortunes. He believed the only protection was to select stocks whose earnings were growing faster than the overall economy.

T. Rowe Price

Additionally, Rowe Price has said he *expects* to pay up for an outstanding growth prospect. This, he defines, is a company whose earnings per share reaches a new high level at the peak of each succeeding major business cycle and which gives indications of reaching new high earnings at the peak of future business cycles.

Rowe Price, an authentic investment genius, has said that the individual investor can duplicate his record *if* "they select well-managed companies in fertile fields for growth and hold the stocks until it's obvious that the company is no longer growing.. and then, and only then, is it time to sell."

Among the growth stocks in the 1930's and 1940's were chemical companies such as DuPont, Dow and Monsanto, and Price's background was ideal for early success. As a former research chemist at DuPont, picking stocks where technology was important came as second nature. His familiarity with the dynamics of technology in chemistry was later easily transferred in the 1950's to the computer and electronics industries where the IBM's and Xerox's were waiting to be discovered.

The selection process, according to Price, is clear cut. His requirements for selecting "T. Rowe Price-type" growth companies have been printed and reprinted in scores of articles and printed interviews over the years. They are:

(1)   A fertile field (industry or business) in which to operate;
(2)   Superior research to develop products and markets;
(3)   A lack of cutthroat competition;
(4)   A comparative immunity from government regulation;
(5)   Low total labor costs, but well-paid employees;
(6)   The promise of a higher-than-average percent return on invested capital, sustained high profit margins, and a superior growth of earnings per share.

Armed with this list, Price notes, the successful investor must take into account the investing environment: the backdrop of social, political, as well as economic influences. The rest is simply sweat and dedication. But Rowe Price is anything but complacent or presumptuous at any given moment in time. His favorite saying, borrowed from the Greeks, but almost his trademark: "Change is the investor's only certainty."

Rowe Price's emphasis on the long-term view is based on the difficulties of successful trading. He views trading as three tough decisions. . .when to buy, when to sell and (presuming one wants to keep money working long term in equities) when to buy again. Another very important reason for his long term view: an investor who pays taxes is usually much better off by staying with a successful stock since taxes are postponed indefinitely. The trader, on the other hand, must pay taxes as well as higher brokerage commissions. The net effect is less money available for investment after each successive sell decision.

Even following his retirement from his namesake firm, T. Rowe Price Associates, Rowe Price never stopped searching for companies in expanding industries where above-average sales and earnings growth could be found. While Price seemed to favor technology where companies stress research, patents and innovation, it was not always the case. Sometimes growth was found in natural resource areas, service industries or retailing.

Once a stock was selected that fit the qualifications of growth, the question was *when* to buy — now or later. Again, Price was not adverse to paying for growth, but he felt there were a few guidelines to follow:

- First, the key valuation of a stock was not asset value per share but present or future earning power per share. The record of the past would give some indication of the future. Where faster growth was projected, a higher multiple of future earnings could be paid. But, he cautioned about projecting earnings growth too far in the future.

- How much you pay for earnings depends on how much can be earned on alternative low-risk investments. In other words, the yields on U.S. Treasury bills would be the minimum base on which to compare returns. Higher interest rates would mean smaller premiums for growth stocks.

- He also felt the best time to buy was when growth stocks were out of fashion.

Finally, once a stock was bought, Price left it alone in his portfolio to do its work. . .as long as progress continued. But nothing goes on forever and Rowe Price was quite willing to sell when earnings growth leveled out. A decline in the rate of return on stockholders' equity would be one of the most important indications.

Much can be learned by studying the accomplishments of T. Rowe Price, for he is one of the few true investment legends to come along in our lifetime.

Benjamin Graham

The late Ben Graham, the father of modern security analysis, and also known as the "Dean" of security analysts, personified the *value* or "bird-in-hand" approach to investing. His emphasis was on current dividend income, tangible asset values, and conservative valuation of earnings. He was also a college professor and a co-author of the classic textbook *Security Analysis*. Its thesis: invest your equity money for "total return" — the sum of dividend plus potential price appreciation.

Ben Graham advocated the value, low P/E approach to investing long before it became fashionable. It was his objective to buy productive assets that could eventually produce earnings. And he wanted to buy those assets as cheaply as possible. Investors, he believed, should buy stocks of profitable companies at a price equal to, or less than, two-thirds of net current asset value. Above all, he sought financial soundness by avoiding companies having excessive debt. By nailing down more dividend yield now, less future price appreciation would be necessary to attain a satisfactory total return; hence, the search for below-average earnings multiples of sound stocks. In addition, there would be an extra bonus if the multiple rises along with earnings. Furthermore, if an investor can buy stock value at a significant discount, so much the better, since the stock could be a takeover candidate.

Once the stock advances 50%, Graham would recommend taking profits and reinvesting the money into another stock meeting the original "value" standards. Of course, unfortunately, most are of small, unknown companies.

It was Graham's opinion that the institutional investor could not, over time, obtain better results than the Dow Jones Industrial Average or the Standard & Poor's Index. "In effect," he said, "that would mean that the stock market experts could best themselves — a logical contradiction." On the other hand, he felt that the typical investor has a great advantage over the large institutions. He believed that investors willing to do a little independent research could outperform the overall market by simply stressing the value approach.

Benjamin Graham

Ralph Coleman

Ralph Coleman, who died at a relatively young age in 1980, was a rare combination — a financial journalist and investment manager. He was founder and president of the Over-The-Counter Securities Fund and the publisher of the *Over-the-Counter Securities Review.*

The investment approach Ralph Coleman advocated was simple and straight-forward: "Buy small bargains!" Moreover, it was his opinion that, for the most part, stocks of this type would most likely be found in the over-the-counter market.

In an interview just before he died, Coleman offered a few opinions regarding the following "rules" widely used on Wall Street:

(1) There is no point trying to buy "well-managed companies" since companies that are widely recognized as such are usually overpriced;

(2) Gerald Loeb always used to say "Cut your losses, but let your profits run." Coleman disagreed by arguing that investors who do this will always find themselves selling good or bad stocks at the bottom;

(3) It is a bad idea to be buying "what the institutions are buying." Coleman maintained that the institutions buy the "hot stocks" after most of the move has taken place;

(4) Buying "big, well-established companies" is not necessarily the answer. Coleman considered companies in this category to be too large for substantial appreciation and often-times mature and "over-the-hill."

Ralph P. Coleman, Sr.

"My fundamental research consists basically of annual reports, quarterlies, and other published material available to everyone," he would say. He, like T. Rowe Price and Ben Graham, spent much time poring over data of unknown companies. The inefficient market segment was, in effect, his "element."

Other "Independent Thinkers"

The list of talented analysts and investment personalities can go on and on. For example, David Baker, president of the 44 Wall Street Fund, has one of the best investment records over the past decade or so. His fund is nearly always among the top five or ten performers in terms of capital appreciation. Basically, his superior record has been compiled by rejecting the notion that "big is beautiful." Instead, he has concentrated on smaller companies. He feels it is almost impossible to call the swings in the market, he is fully invested most of the time and he favors business sectors and companies with higher-than-average earnings growth prospects.

Another example is one of the best investment managers on the West Coast, Claude N. Rosenberg, Jr., who made has mark in the 1960's in growth stocks when he was head of research of a regional brokerage firm. He went on to found the highly successful Rosenberg Capital Management, Inc. which manages billions of institutional and pension fund dollars.

Among Claude Rosenberg's early successes were small growth companies, which he called "bikini" stocks, named after the small bathing suit. When related to growth companies, however, it meant explosive potential earning power, coupled with a small amount of stock outstanding.

Claude Rosenberg's view is that large companies with huge capitalizations must develop a constant stream of new products to fuel large earnings increases. On the other hand, a single product or service in a "bikini" company would result in an immediate and magnified effect on earnings and on the stock price. Rosenberg has always been quick to point out the reverse can also be true. A product that fails to meet expectations can have a disasterous effect on earnings. . .and perhaps on a company's solvency as well.

Finally, there is John Westergaard, the "guru" of junior growth stocks. He is president of Equity Research Associates, an organization specializing in the research of small-sized companies having the potential for substantial sales and earnings growth.

The companies followed by Westergaard and his associates are defined as industrial, service, and specialty retail companies of a size that generally fall below the *"Fortune* 1,000" (the magazine's list of the country's largest 1,000 firms). Among the data they (as do most analysts) monitor closely: sales growth, earnings per share growth, price earnings ratios, growth rates over the past five years, return on equity, debt relative to shareholders' equity, and the annual dividend rate per share.

Like T. Rowe Price and David Babson, Westergaard searches for companies in "fertile fields of growth." He calls them market "niches," which are often too small, at least in the early years, to be exploited by the giants of industry.

In addition, Westergaard is looking for:

- A special management. Frequently, these are people who have left other well-managed companies to become entrepreneurs. In addition, this management will have demonstrated a company strategy and direction.

- The development or application of a new technology or a new technique of doing business; or the evolution of consumer spending patterns. In any case, the prospect should be in a position of leadership in its industry or sub-industry.

- An ability to obtain capital over the next five years. This, he maintains, is tied directly to the company's profitability and return on equity. The companies favored usually have a high return on equity — perhaps 25-30% — and, therefore, much of their needed capital will be internally-generated from earnings.

John Westergaard uses the New Horizons Fund of T. Rowe Price Associates as an indicator of junior growth stock valuation, (which he refers to as the "T. Rowe Price 2:1 rule"). This "rule," in effect, compares the P/E ratio of the New Horizons Fund to the P/E ratio of the Standard & Poor's 500 index. Accordingly, whenever the P/E of the fund is twice that of the S & P index, small growth stocks can be considered over-priced.

In an interview with Louis Rukeyser on "Wall Street Week" a year or so ago, Westergaard presented an optimistic look into the 1980's and identified three broad investment categories in which small growth stocks might be found in the future: the first he calls the *Business Frontier* (the development or application of new technology or new techniques of doing business); second, *American Lifestyles* (the evolution of consumer spending patterns); and, finally, *Special Situations* (miscellaneous opportunities).

Although it may be years before we can judge whether John Westergaard's optimism is justified, his past record suggests that we should be listening.

That Magic Combination

Small is definitely beautiful when it comes to achieving the kind of growth rate that will eventually produce a super stock. For example, the opening of a new market niche may not even budge the net earnings of a company with more than $500 million dollars in revenues, but that same new market could conceivably double the net earnings of a $50 million company. (And one definition of a super stock is "A company whose earnings will increase at a rate of at least 50% greater than the current level of long-term interest rates.") To generate these earnings, the super stock candidate will typically pay only a small dividend to its shareholders, preferring to reinvest the bulk of each year's earnings into new product development, new plant and equipment, or to increase the market penetration of existing products. This, in turn, will increase profitability and generate larger amounts of profits which will then be reinvested to generate still more profits. Like the ram-jet engine, the faster the jet goes, the more air to be taken in and compressed, thus propelling the jet even faster through the air. And so will it be for our super stock. More money will be made to invest in new plant and equipment to produce more products at a still higher profit. . .which will be reinvested again. . .and so on.

After a time, this continued compounding of earnings will eventually be recognized in the marketplace. At that point, the consistency of earnings growth becomes a highly predictable event encouraging investors to appraise the stock at significantly higher prices. For an investor holding a super stock, dramatic earnings growth coupled with an expanding P/E multiple can be a truly magic combination.

Fast Growth From A Smaller Company

The compounding effect of sales and earnings can have a profound impact on the long term results of any growth investment — especially if a rapid growth rate can be maintained for an extended period of time. However, growth can also become more difficult to attain as the business gets larger. This point is dramatically illustrated by this example: A company with sales of $50 million, and facing five years of 30% annual growth, must add $55 million to its sales base in the sixth year to continue its growth rate of 30%! Some can do it; many others cannot.

Therefore, logic tells us, it would seem easier for a $50 million business to double in size than it would be for one $500 million large. So, in the Wall Street arena, what is a "big" or "small" company? It depends. There is no clear answer, although an investor usually considers himself closer to the "ground floor" with a $5 million enterprise than with, say, a $500 million company.

Moreover, the term "size" has a different meaning within each industry. A $100 million publishing company is quite large; a $100 million oil services company is fairly small. And, while the management of Chrysler might not agree, other problems, such as financing, might be more difficult for a $5 million company than for a firm ten, twenty, or a hundred times its size. Of course, this is not to imply that problems of financing are peculiar only to smaller companies. But credit-worthiness, which frequently comes with maturity, is by far the most important factor.

Our objective is now to identify the optimum size for investment...a company with an ability to finance itself with internally-generated funds and one that has reached a certain sustainability within its own markets. A rapidly-growing company that is too small can go unnoticed by the stock market for years. On the other hand, if the business has reached such a size that a significant portion of its entire market(or an entire new market) must be added just to maintain its earlier growth rate, the company has probably already passed its super stock stage.

As we pore through our library data, what, then, is the ideal size of our super-stock-to-be? *Experience suggests that companies with sales in the range of $25 million to $500 million should be given priority in the analysis.* Does this mean that IBM, with $734 million sales in 1956, or Eastman Kodak, with $633 million in 1954, were bad selections? Of course not. Or would it have been wrong to buy Capital Cities Broadcasting in 1963 when sales were only $17 million? No! There are no hard and fast rules on Wall Street.

Generally speaking, companies in this $25 million to $500 million range have the best of all worlds. By this time, they have "made it" in their respective markets and, at the same time, they are still small enough to enjoy significant growth. But how can potential earnings growth be gauged?

In corporate finance, the compounding effect on earnings can be measured by the *earned growth rate*; the annual rate at which the stockholders' equity or capital is increased. Stockholders' capital are those corporate assets left after deducting debt and preferred liabilities. Stockholders' equity is also synonymous with "book value."

To demonstrate the effectiveness of the build-up in stockholders' equity where a company's earnings are growing rapidly and (due to a modest dividend payout) are allowed to compound, let's take a mythical company, ABC Corporation, which has the following characteristics:

- Earnings per share growing at 20% a year, compounded;
- A dividend on common shares that is fixed at a 20% payout of earnings; and
- A current book value of $10 per share.

To calculate the effect of compounding, we use the per share book value at the beginning of the year since this is what the ABC Corporation executives had with which to work. To get our *earned growth rate*, we use the earnings per share for the year ended, less the dividend paid to stockholders. What's left is plowed back into the corporation for investment. The "plowback" in earnings is then divided by the book value at the beginning of the year to give us an earned growth rate percentage.

The formula is:

$$\text{Earned Growth Rate } = \frac{\text{Annual earnings } less \text{ annual dividends}}{\text{Book value (beginning of the year)}}$$

Using this formula we can see how ABC Corporation's book value builds up:

Year	Beginning Value	Earnings	Dividends	"Plow Back"	Earned Growth Rate	Return on Stockholders' Equity*
1	$10.00	$ 1.00	$ .20	$ .80	8.0%	10.0%
2	10.80	1.20	.24	.96	8.9	11.1
3	11.76	1.44	.29	1.15	9.8	12.2
4	12.91	1.73	.35	1.38	10.7	13.4
5	14.29	2.08	.42	1.66	11.6	14.6
6	15.95	2.50	.50	2.00	12.5	15.7
7	17.95	3.00	.60	2.40	13.4	16.7
8	20.35	3.60	.72	2.88	14.2	17.7
9	23.23	4.32	.86	3.46	14.9	18.6
10	26.69	5.18	1.04	4.14	15.5	19.4

*To be precise, it is better to calculate ROE by dividing the earnings figure by the *average* of beginning and ending book values.

Let's assume that in year one the common stock was selling at $10 a share, right on book value since ABC Corporation was little known to investors. Put another way, at $10 a share, the investor was buying $1 in earnings; a price earnings multiple of *10*. Consider that even if the stock continued to sell at *book value...* and nothing else...our equity per share would increase 167% in ten years, tax free to the stockholder! But remember, investors often disregard book value—they buy earnings. So while equity rose 167%, earnings moved from $1.00 to $5.18 per share in ten years. Assuming investors paid no more than ten times earnings, our stock price would rise from $10.00 to more than $51; an increase of more than 400%! But given the demonstrated earnings record of 20% compounded over a ten year period—investors would probably appraise the stock at a higher multiple since a significant element of predictability has been indicated. A 20% growth rate might call for a multiple of 20 times (or more in enthusiastic markets). Applying a P/E of 20 to our 10th year earnings per share of $5.18, we could see a price of $103.60! Actually, at this point, investors would probably be looking into an 11th year of 20% earnings increase--an expected earnings of $6.22 per share. So our ABC Corporation stock in the 10th year could be selling at 20 x $6.22 or $124.40, an increase of 1140%!

A company in this $25 million to $500 million range is also much more likely to achieve dramatic results from plowback because it is still at an early stage in its corporate growth cycle. Large, blue-chip companies have long since passed the furious growth of their corporate youth.

The Life Cycle

As we search for super stocks, we're asking ourselves what every football scout asks: Where is the next superstar? He searches the colleges, looking for performance statistics that will reveal the one player who can, almost overnight, "make it" in the Pros. So too, with our search. We want a young, emerging firm with the potential to make it big—to become a large, very profitable company. We want to catch the company early when the stock price does not yet fully reflect its future earnings potential.

Although life cycles vary by company and by industry, the growth curve shown on the next page reflects the largest part of corporate experience.

The Life Cycle of a Company

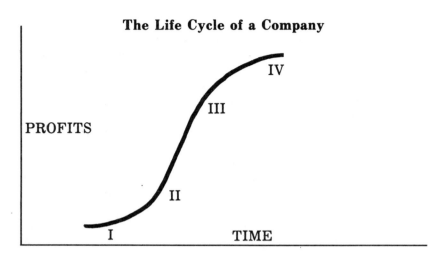

PHASE I *A NEW VENTURE!*

During the development period, the company pays little, if any, dividends to the stockholders. Most of the money invested in the company to date as been from the founders and venture capitalists. Profit margins are generally low, or perhaps non-existent at this stage.

PHASE II *THE EARLY YEARS: RAPID GROWTH*

Growth has begun and the company's profitability is becoming more evident. Profit margins are climbing and the earnings "plowback" is now financing most of the company's needs for capital. Small cash or stock dividends are declared. The company and the stock are becoming recognized!

PHASE III *CONTINUED GROWTH*

The company's profitability is now reaching its peak. Plants are being built to meet the heavy product demand. Competition is becoming more evident. Dividend increases and stock splits are almost commonplace. Now the company is a leader in its field.

PHASE IV *MATURITY*

Sharp increases in sales are becoming infrequent. At this point, either the new products developed during Phase III are starting to make a contribution or a decline is beginning to set in. Cash dividends are now a larger portion of earnings — perhaps 50% or more of annual profits. Competition is now much more intense and, while earnings may still be increasing, profit margins are declining. Analysts and brokers are currently calling the stock "a 'core holding' for long term portfolios."

If this effort is successful, we could be in a position to do what many "experienced" investors only dream of doing: to buy low and sell high. The following exhibit is the actual experience of a well-known super stock several years ago.

The Life Cycle of One Super Stock: A Real Life Story

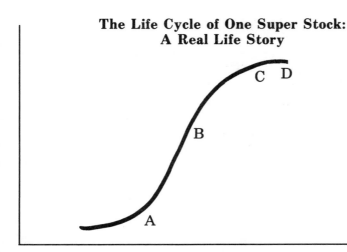

A
Year: 1
Sales: $65.3 million
Profit Margin: 24.5%
EPS: $0.23
Dividend: $0.03
Stock Price: 9 1/2
P/E Ratio: 41.3

Sales + 36% from last year; EPS + 28%; Dividends + 50%. P/E expanded from 27 to 41 times earnings; stock nearly double the price of last year.
Minor institutional interest.

B
Year: 8
Sales: $204.0 million
Profit Margin: 28.3%
EPS: $0.93
Dividend: $0.06
Stock Price: 43 3/8
P/E Ratio: 46.6

Sales + 46% from last year; EPS + 60%; Dividends + 100%. The P/E multiple is advancing and the stock is being accumulated by institutions.

C
Year: 12
Sales: $465.6 million
Profit Margin: 27.6%
EPS: $1.92
Dividend: $0.32
Stock Price: 124 1/8
P/E Ratio: 64.6

Sales + 16% from last year; EPS + 3%; Dividend unchanged from prior year; Profit margins peaked in year 11 at 31%. Institutions own the stock heavily.

D
Year: 13
Sales: $444.3 million
Profit Margin: 25.6%
EPS: $1.86
Dividend: $0.32
Stock Price: 90 7/8
P/E Ratio: 48.9

This was the first of many disappointing years. Several years later, record sales and earnings were reported, but the stock price and the P/E of this "growth stock emeritus" settled at substantially lower levels.

An Expanding P/E Multiple

One of the most widely used (some say over-used) valuation tools on Wall Street is the *Price Earnings Ratio*, also variously called the "P/E ratio" the "P/E Multiple," or just simply the "P/E" or "The Multiple." By whatever name, it is a constantly-varying, sometimes mysterious relationship between the stock's price and its earnings per share. Strictly speaking, the P/E is calculated by dividing the earnings per share into the stock price. Usually, the EPS figure is of the latest 12-month period. However, it is not an uncommon practice to calculate the multiple on earnings estimated 12 months into the future (this seems especially true when stocks are rising and analysts and portfolio managers are feeling more courageous). Nor would it be an understatement to say that an entire book can be devoted to explaining the P/E multiple. The variables can boggle the mind.

The table on the next page demonstrates the important role P/E's played in five now-classic "round trips." As the figures show, when earnings are growing, an expanding P/E can result in fantastic price performance! But a rich multiple and an earnings disappointment can be as dramatic as a free-falling safe from the tenth floor.

BRUNSWICK CORPORATION

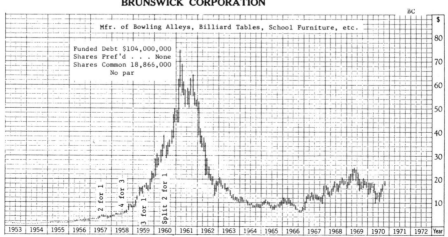

Avon Products	1955	1973	1974
Stock Price	1 3/8	140	18 5/8
EPS	0.11	2.34	1.92
P/E	12.5	59.8	9.7
% Contribution: Earnings	—	20%	21%
P/E	—	80%	79%
Brunswick Corporation	**1956**	**1961**	**1962**
Stock Price	2 1/2	74 7/8	13 1/8
EPS	0.37	2.56	1.36
P/E	6.8	29.2	9.7
%Contribution: Earnings	—	21%	57%
P/E	—	79%	43%
Fleetwood Enterprises	**1967**	**1972**	**1973**
Stock Price	2 5/8	49 1/2	3 1/2
EPS	0.18	1.21	0.44
P/E	14.6	40.9	8.0
% Contribution: Earnings	—	32%	68%
P/E	—	68%	32%
Holiday Inns	**1964**	**1972**	**1974**
Stock Price	4 1/8	55 5/8	4 1/4
EPS	0.21	1.38	1.06
P/E	19.6	40.3	4.0
% Contribution: Earnings	—	45%	25%
P/E	—	55%	75%
Polaroid Corporation	**1957**	**1969**	**1974**
Stock Price	5 3/8	145 3/4	14 1/8
EPS	0.18	1.92	0.86
P/E	29.9	75.9	16.4
% Contribution: Earnings	—	37%	61%
P/E	—	63%	39%

No discussion on P/E multiples is complete without an answer to the question: "At what price?" Without becoming inextricably involved in a subject no less perplexing than the meaning of life itself, there is one valuation approach worthy of note. The table on the next page (reproduced with permission; *Understanding Wall Street;* Liberty Publishing Company, 1982), is based on a revised version of a formula developed by the late Benjamin Graham, the "Dean" of security analysts.

To use this table, the investor must first estimate the company's annual growth rate for the next 7 to 10 years. Then, by crossing this growth rate with the prevailing interest rate for Aaa bonds, the table will reveal a P/E multiple that can be used as a starting point to any analysis.

Price/Earnings Ratios Assuming Different Growth Rates and Interest Rates

Prevailing Interest Rate

Expected Growth Rate	3%	4%	5%	6%	7%	8%	9%	10%	11%	12%	13%	14%	15%	16%	17%	18%
20%	71.2	53.4	42.7	35.6	30.5	26.7	23.7	21.4	19.4	17.8	16.4	15.3	14.2	13.3	12.6	11.9
19%	68.2	51.2	40.9	34.1	29.2	25.6	22.7	20.5	18.6	17.1	15.7	14.6	13.6	12.8	12.0	11.4
18%	65.3	49.0	39.2	32.7	28.0	24.5	21.8	19.6	17.8	16.3	15.1	14.0	13.1	12.2	11.5	10.9
17%	62.4	46.8	37.4	31.2	26.7	23.4	20.8	18.7	17.0	15.6	14.4	13.4	12.5	11.7	11.0	10.4
16%	59.4	44.6	35.7	29.7	25.5	22.3	19.8	17.8	16.2	14.9	13.7	12.7	11.9	11.1	10.5	9.9
15%	56.5	42.4	33.9	28.3	24.2	21.2	18.8	17.0	15.4	14.1	13.0	12.1	11.3	10.6	10.0	9.4
14%	53.6	40.2	32.1	26.8	23.0	20.1	17.9	16.1	14.6	13.4	12.4	11.5	10.7	10.0	9.5	8.9
13%	50.6	38.0	30.4	25.3	21.7	19.0	16.9	15.2	13.8	12.7	11.7	10.9	10.1	9.5	8.9	8.4
12%	47.7	35.8	28.6	23.9	20.4	17.9	15.9	14.3	13.0	11.9	11.0	10.2	9.5	8.9	8.4	8.0
11%	44.8	33.6	26.9	22.4	19.2	16.8	14.9	13.4	12.2	11.2	10.3	9.6	9.0	8.4	7.9	7.5
10%	41.8	31.4	25.1	20.9	17.9	15.7	13.9	12.6	11.4	10.5	9.7	9.0	8.4	7.8	7.4	7.0
9%	38.9	29.2	23.3	19.5	16.7	14.6	13.0	11.7	10.6	9.7	9.0	8.3	7.8	7.3	6.9	6.5
8%	36.0	27.0	21.6	18.0	15.4	13.5	12.0	10.8	9.8	9.0	8.3	7.7	7.2	6.7	6.3	6.0
7%	33.0	24.8	19.8	16.5	14.2	12.4	11.0	9.9	9.0	8.3	7.6	7.1	6.6	6.2	5.8	5.5
6%	30.1	22.6	18.1	15.1	12.9	11.3	10.0	9.0	8.2	7.5	6.9	6.5	6.0	5.6	5.3	5.0
5%	27.2	20.4	16.3	13.6	11.6	10.2	9.1	8.2	7.4	6.8	6.3	5.8	5.4	5.1	4.8	4.5
4%	24.3	18.2	14.5	12.1	10.4	9.1	8.1	7.3	6.6	6.1	5.6	5.2	4.8	4.5	4.3	4.0
3%	21.3	16.0	12.8	10.7	9.1	8.0	7.1	6.4	5.8	5.3	4.9	4.6	4.3	4.0	3.8	3.6

Learning From The Past

Each year there are stocks that do better than the stock market averages; in many cases, spectacularly better. More importantly, there are stocks that year-in and year-out outperform the market as a whole in good as well as bad markets. Each year we read articles about how one investor made a million dollars buying Stock A or Stock B or using a new failure-proof technique.

As one Wall Street expert used to say when asked about investing success:

"Making money in the stock market is simply to have stock you bought at lower levels go up dramatically in price and stay there. . . ."

Wouldn't you have loved to have bought Scientific Atlanta at 2 or 3 during the depths of the bear market of 1974 and watched the stock move dramatically up more than ten-fold in the next few years! Remember Walt Disney, Xerox, McDonald's, or Houston Oil and Minerals? These stocks all went up anywhere from 8 to 20 times their buying price over five and ten year periods in the past. Few of the great stock performers were new issues. . .and all these companies were in different industries. . .oil, technology, fast food. They also possessed different management styles.

Basically, the companies that made investors big money were neither very small nor very large, but something in between. The trick was to identify these companies at their "take-off" stage where the company was clearly demonstrating its ability to generate high cash profits in a growing area of activity. This is the point where you can identify a super stock and buy it cheap because most investors have not yet found it.

Year in and year out, brokers innundate investors with lists of recommended stocks. They offer stocks selling at substantial discounts from book value where ratios of recent price to tangible asset values are low (that is, they appear cheap compared to market averages); or stocks with the high dividend returns; or stocks with the lowest price earnings ratios. All these recommendations are interesting and probably of some use, but the astute investor looking for maximum appreciation will realize that:

- Discounted corporate assets are of little value unless someone else wants them at a higher price, or new management has a way to utilize those assets into producing greater earnings. After all, in the final analysis, that's what assets are for: to produce income.
- Dividends are, indeed, extremely important, as this chapter later illustrates. However, dividends are merely the *result* of earnings, secondary in importance to the plowback of earnings for continued growth. Further, dividends represent two taxes. The first is paid by the corporation; the second is later paid by the shareholder who receives the dividends.
- Low price earnings ratios (low, relative to other stocks, that is) may represent earning power at a bargain...but that's rarely the case. Usually, low price earnings ratios, particularly if they've been low for a long period of time represent the stock market's sensing of cut-throat competition, inordinate government regulation, an industry that is declining rather than growing and so on...

What does work if these methods don't?

Most of the answer lies in the past. Which stocks have done well over long periods of time and why? The same stocks and the same industries rarely repeat...but the companies behind the super stocks hold some lessons that can be useful in the future. To this end, a list was compiled of many high performing stocks, in terms of capital appreciation, over the past few decades. The review included stocks of all kinds, listed or over-the-counter. The only qualification was that they be readily available for purchase by an investor.

By reviewing the winners of past decades, it was possible to identify those common characteristics these achievers seem to possess, and then to analyze and test those characteristics to the point where they could be used in sifting through thousands of stocks to identify future "super stocks."

The universe of common stocks was screened to select those that performed best in recent history. Performance meant maximum capital gains during the period studied. Once these stocks were identified, a review of their operating history was undertaken to determine what specific quantitative and qualitative factors appeared most frequently in all of the stocks. It was also necessary to determine when the identification of those factors could have been put to best use during the upward price movement of the stock.

The review encompassed the years since World War II and continued through recent years. Logically, this time period seemed to divide itself into two segments: from the end of World War II to the beginning of the Vietnam build-up in 1965; and, from 1966 to the present. The 1930's, for example, was a recovery economy characterized by fledgling government support and tax programs. And, although the 1920's featured economic expansion, that era of liberalism and unfettered business activity ended decisively with the 1929 crash and the economic chaos that followed.

The Post-War Era

The Post-War era was characterized by consecutively high periods of commodity inflation (1945, 1946) accompanied by persistently low price earnings ratios (also, see Appendix "B"), followed by a war expansion (Korea 1950-1953). Shortly thereafter, the country saw another recession and low inflation and even lower interest rates. Then, in the late 50's, the economy turned upward and price earnings ratios advanced sharply. This era ended with the enormous build-up of national budget deficits to finance social programs and to fight the war in Vietnam. These deficits and the huge increase in the money supply that followed were soon reflected in surging inflation and interest rates.

The ten-year period following the 1957-58 recession produced many stocks which performed dramatically and persist to this day as viable investments (although most have already passed through the "super stock" stage of their lives). For the shrewd investor, 1958 was a good year to invest. Corporate earnings and stocks were down, pessimism was rampant, and, in general, prices did not appear cheap.

In the next table, ten selected stocks are listed alphabetically along with the 1958 markets from which each might have been identified as a prime capital gains candidate. Also shown are the earnings and dividends in 1958 and, again, ten years later. The 1958 stock prices shown were obtainable at the time. The 1968 price is that of the original stock without adjusting for stock splits or dividends.

This table illustrates the important role sharply higher earnings and P/E multiples can play in a super stock portfolio. The higher stock price resulting is, of course, the investor's primary objective. However, the added benefit of growing dividends should not be overlooked. The table shows, for example, that the meager $2.60 IBM dividend in 1958 grew to a more-respectable 5.4% annual return by 1968. Today, those same investors are enjoying a 30% return each year on that original investment. And, incredible as it may seem, Xerox investors are receiving, annually, nearly THREE TIMES their original investment. . .just from the dividend alone.

Clearly, dividend growth of this magnitude would not have been possible without the reinvestment (plowback) of profits in earlier years. Yet, when reviewing the table, the high payout ratio of Emery Air Freight stands out. How can a company grow as rapidly as Emery and still pay such a generous dividend at the same time? The answer is simple, after a little analysis. During this period, Emery was primarily a service business without serious competition, not very capital-intensive, and without the need to own much equipment. Therefore, the company's return on equity was very high (47% in 1968) which permitted a generous payout during those years. As long as Emery's ROE remained high, investors could expect a healthy earned growth rate *and* generous dividends.

DIVIDEND RETURNS FROM
SELECTED HIGH PERFORMANCE STOCKS
(1958-1968)

Company	Where Traded in 1958	Avg. Price 1958	1958 EPS	1958 Div.	1958 Yield	Avg. Price 1968	1968 EPS	1968 Div.	% of Original Investment
Avon Products	OTC	$ 61	$ 3.36	$1.45	2.4%	$1,169	$ 22.32	$14.40	23.5%
Baxter Products	OTC	32	2.42	0.74	2.3%	705	13.28	2.72	8.4%
Black & Decker	NYSE	48	3.16	1.70	3.6%	322	12.90	6.30	13.2%
Bristol-Myers	NYSE	65	4.38	2.15	3.3%	857	23.52	13.20	20.1%
Emery Air Freight	ASE	15	0.72	0.55	3.6%	266	5.76	3.72	24.4%
International Business Machines	NYSE	426	10.65	2.60	0.6%	2,903	68.35	23.04	5.4%
Johnson & Johnson	NYSE	116	5.95	2.05	1.8%	684	20.48	4.88	4.2%
Minnesota Mining & Manufacturing	NYSE	95	2.58	1.20	1.3%	301	8.91	4.35	4.6%
Nalco Chemical	OTC	37	2.83	1.25	3.4%	405	10.64	4.24	11.5%
Xerox (Haloid)	OTC	72	1.96	0.80	1.1%	5,576	103.80	28.80	40.1%

Recall the *Earned Growth Rate* formula from Chapter III:

$$\text{Earned Growth Rate} = \frac{\text{Annual earnings } \textit{less} \text{ annual dividends}}{\text{Book value (beginning of the year)}}$$

Here, then, is another definition of a super stock: "A company showing a return on equity high enough to eventually produce significant dividends."

The Post-1966 Period

The year 1966 was selected as the starting point of the second period since it marked the beginning of the inflation speed-up that created a host of problems in the 1970's and early 1980's. This period was a difficult one for most companies. It was punctuated in 1973-1974 by a quadrupling of oil prices, double-digit inflation, rising interest rates and a sharp recession. Even so, companies exhibiting rising earnings usually had those earnings reflected in rising stock prices despite all the economic problems of the period. The deep recession and stock market decline of 1974 set the stage for a whole new group of companies oriented toward natural resources or in new industries unthought of in the 1960's.

Among top market performers of the post-1966 period were the following seven representative stocks. Most enjoyed a substantial recovery from the lows of 1974.

Name	Where Traded	1966 Cost	1972 High	1974 Low	Recent Value
Block (H&R)	OTC•NYSE	$21	$420	$ 53	$ 380
Cox Broadcasting	NYSE	35	102	18	288
Digital Equipment	OTC•ASE•NYSE	26	309	147	783
Hewlett-Packard	NYSE	46	176	104	320
McDonald's Corp.	OTC•NYSE	25	963	269	812
Schlumberger	NYSE	50	425	331	1,276
Tandy Corp.	NYSE	15	98	20	2,176

Note: Prices are unadjusted for stock splits.

SCHLUMBERGER, LTD.

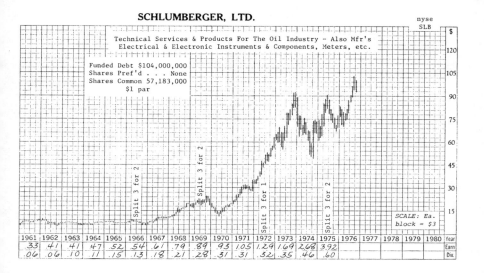

nyse
SLB

Technical Services & Products For The Oil Industry – Also Mfr's
Electrical & Electronic Instruments & Components, Meters, etc.

Funded Debt $104,000,000
Shares Pref'd . . . None
Shares Common 57,183,000
$1 par

SCALE: Ea.
block = $3

Year	1961	1962	1963	1964	1965	1966	1967	1968	1969	1970	1971	1972	1973	1974	1975	1976	1977	1978	1979	1980
Earn	.33	.41	.41	.47	.52	.54	.61	.79	.89	.93	1.05	1.29	1.69	2.68	3.92					
Div.	.06	.06	.10	.11	.15	.13	.18	.21	.28	.31	.31	.32	.35	.46	.60					

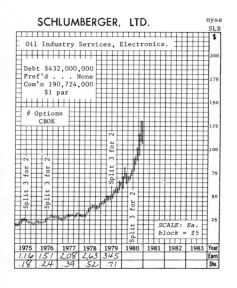

SCHLUMBERGER, LTD.

nyse
SLB

Oil Industry Services, Electronics.

Debt $432,000,000
Pref'd . . . None
Com'n 190,724,000
$1 par

Options
CBOE

SCALE: Ea.
block = $5

Year	1975	1976	1977	1978	1979	1980	1981	1982	1983
Earn	1.16	1.51	2.08	2.63	3.45				
Div.	.18	.24	.39	.52	.71				

Schlumberger (pronouced Schlum-ber-shay) stock proved to be one of the big winners of the 1970's, rising nearly 2,000% in ten years. Clearly, this oil service company was at the right place at the right time!

TANDY CORPORATION

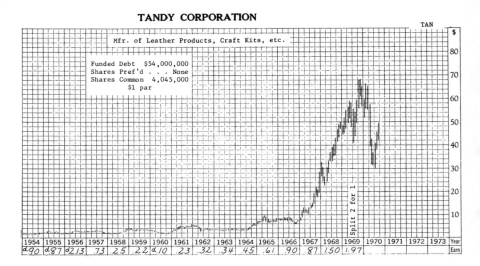

Look closely at both Tandy charts. Notice how an investor's perspective
can change with time. The frightening 1969-70 plunge lost its significance
in later years. By 1982, the stock was nearly $80 ($640 before adjusting for
splits since 1969)!

TANDY CORPORATION

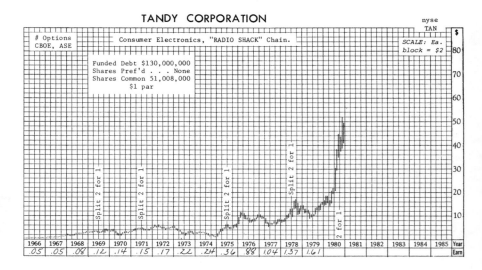

But not all that glitters is gold. Here are a few of the "new" growth stocks of the 1960's that became the "busts" even before the great bear market of the 1970's:

Growth Stars of the Sixties

	1960-70 High	Market Price September, 1972
Alpine Geophysical	44	1 3/4
Ampex	49 7/8	6 3/8
Arlan's Department Stores	40 7/8	3 1/2
Ecological Science	28 3/4	Trading Suspended
Electronic Memories	43 3/4	4 1/8
FAS International	82	1/8
Four Seasons Nursing	102	Trading Suspended
Ionics	61 1/2	16 3/4
Ipco Hospital Supply	37 3/4	8 7/8
Leasco	57 1/4	21 5/8
L-T-V	169 1/2	10
Management Assistance	45	3/8
Mattel	52	14 7/8
Memorex	174	17 7/8
National Student Marketing	79	3/4
Potter Instruments	46	9 1/4
Pueblo International	26 3/8	6 7/8
Savin Business Machines	73	15 3/4
Tyco	68	16 3/8
University Computing	187	13 3/8

The tabulation is more eloquent than thousands of words regarding the "buy and hold" strategy which claims that all you have to do is identify, buy, and then hold a growth stock to become rich. What the experts were saying in the early 1970's was that established growth records are usually good buys for the long pull even if their price earnings ratios are high. That's fine as long as the company is still growing rapidly. Of course, few of these ever met our super stock qualifications in the first place.

One of the more memorable "busts" began in late 1972—Levitz Furniture, one of the so-called "concept" stocks of the early 1970's. It was the first company with a new type of retailing: combination warehouse-showroom-retail stores which sold nationally-advertised brands of furniture. These products were priced lower than in conventional furniture stores and the stores were big, with plenty of showroom and warehouse space. It was an innovative selling tool in a hide-bound industry. The results were spectacular in the furniture business and in the stock market. The stock could have been purchased at 13 in January, 1971. It quickly rose to 60 in mid-1972. You had to be quick, though. The stock stopped abruptly and then declined to a low of 17 that same year. It eventually hit 2 in 1974. Levitz may have been a growth company of sorts, but it could not maintain the earnings power it took years to build in a traditionally low-margin business with rising competition and difficult economic times.

These experiences provide yet another definition of super stock: "A stock that is rising for sound, long term fundamental reasons; not just a temporary move in a bull market." Most importantly, we are seeking a sustainability of earning power, not just a "flash in the pan." We are looking for more than just a super price-performance; we want stocks at "never-again" prices!

Finally, looking back over the past thirty or forty years, there is still one more lesson to be learned: *Super stocks can be found at any time.* For example, the five years between 1976 and 1982 were not especially bright for the stock market. During these years, the U.S. encountered a recession, inflation and unemployment rose to extremely high levels, the prime rate climbed above 20%, and U.S. prestige hit its lowest point when its embassy was overrun by a second-rate country. In 1976, the Dow Jones Industrial Average high was 1027. Not surprisingly, the index stood at 875 at the end of 1981, about 15% lower. However, during this same period, the stock of an automation equipment company called Computervision Corporation advanced more than 4,000%. A $2,000 investment in Computervision at its highest price in 1976 had a market value of $85,300 as 1981 drew to a close.

— IBM —

IBM is, of course, one of the premier super stocks. In the mid 1920's, an investor could have bought shares in a growing company called Computing-Tabulating-Recording. At that time, this fledgling office supplier had 120,000 shares outstanding. Today, that company is IBM, a business that made millions for its shareholders. For example, an investor purchasing IBM at the highest price in 1957, before a sharp 25% decline later that year, would have paid $376½ (a P/E of 48.7). In 1957, about 30% of IBM's $7.73 earnings per share was paid to shareholders in dividends. Not adjusting for splits (there have been no fewer than seven since then), IBM stock reached $3,081 in February, 1973! The annual dividend rate currently is equivalent to $145 per share on the stock purchased in 1957. . .a 39% return on the original investment EACH YEAR!

Over the years, IBM's stock rose for sound, long term fundamental reasons. The company moved from a small, fast-growing office equipment manufacturer into the then new field of computers in the early 1950's. Management made a superb bet by concentrating on building a marketing and service

INTERNATIONAL BUSINESS MACHINES

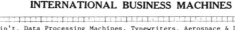

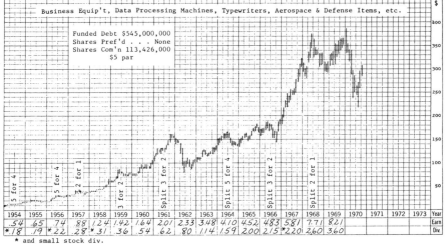

Business Equip't, Data Processing Machines, Typewriters, Aerospace & Defense Items, etc.

Funded Debt $545,000,000
Shares Pref'd . . . None
Shares Com'n 113,426,000
$5 par

Year	1954	1955	1956	1957	1958	1959	1960	1961	1962	1963	1964	1965	1966	1967	1968	1969	1970	1971	1972	1973
Earn	.54	.65	.74	.88	1.24	1.42	1.64	2.01	2.33	3.48	4.10	4.52	4.83	5.81	7.71	8.21				
Div.	*.18	.19	*.22	.28	*.31	.36	.54	.62	.80	1.14	1.59	2.00	2.15	*2.20	2.60	3.60				

* and small stock div.

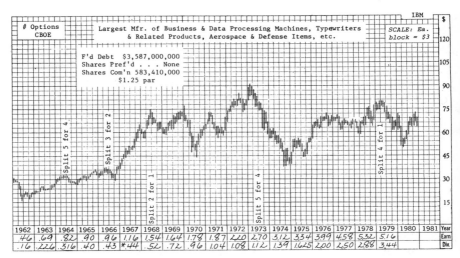

Year	1962	1963	1964	1965	1966	1967	1968	1969	1970	1971	1972	1973	1974	1975	1976	1977	1978	1979	1980	1981
Earn	.46	.69	.82	.90	.96	1.16	1.54	1.64	1.78	1.87	2.20	2.70	3.12	3.34	3.99	4.58	5.32	5.16		
Div.	.16	.226	.316	.40	.43	*44	.52	.72	.96	1.04	1.08	1.12	1.39	1.625	2.00	2.50	2.88	3.44		

organization for IBM equipment. The company soon established dominance. The fact that the computer business proved to
be one of the fastest growing industry segments of the post
World War II period only confirmed management's brilliant
moves and enhanced the results.

And, as these two charts illustrate, a stockholder can benefit
when the P/E multiple is stable or expanding (as it did in the
1954 to 1969 period when IBM earnings grew at 20% per year).
After 1969, earnings continued to grow, but at a slower rate
of 12% annually, and the stock did nothing. That "magic combination" is important. When a company is in its slow-down
(maturity) phase, a shrinking P/E multiple can hurt long term
investment performance.

Few market observers are unaware of the fact that a P/E
of 40 in 1982 was a much more rare phenomenon than it was
ten years earlier. The reasons, the experts tell us, are many —
higher interest rates, higher inflation, slower earnings growth,
etc., etc. At this writing, one thing seems reasonably certain:
the overall direction of most P/E multiples will be more
favorable in the 1980's than it was in the 1970's, which augers
well for future super stock investors. While absolute levels
of P/E's are certainly not to be ignored, it is the TREND, up
or down, that will greatly influence the final results.

— 3M —

Minnesota Mining & Manufacturing started tenuously in 1902 as a venture to quarry a mineral called Corundum at Crystal Bay, Minnesota. The material was then to be sold to eastern manufacturers for use as a new, improved abrasive. After the company's near-failure, Edgar B. Ober and Lucius P. Ordway converted an old flour mill into a sandpaper manufacturing facility. By 1906, the new enterprise was finally enjoying its initial orders, although Corundum was eventually proved worthless as a commercial abrasive.

3M's first plant located on the shore of Lake Superior at Crystal Bay, Minnesota.

William L. McKnight was hired as assistant bookkeeper in May, 1907. At age 24 in 1911, he was appointed sales manager and, soon thereafter, general manager. In 1914, sales were more than $200,000 and climbing due to innovative sales programs instituted by McKnight. "Talk to the people using our sandpaper," he would say. William McKnight was a major force in the company during its first fifty years.

The reorganization instituted by Chief Executive McKnight in 1948 set the stage for substantial growth in the 1950's and beyond. That year, the company was divided into seven major divisions: Adhesives, Roofing Granules, Coated Abrasives, Pressure-Sensitive Tapes, Reflective Products, Color and Chemical, and Electrical Insulation/Sound-Recording Tapes. This company's continuing success over the years has been, in part, due to its corporate organization. To this day, 3M views itself as a collection of many small growth businesses rather than one huge enterprise.

William L. McKnight (2nd from left) welcomes employees to the board room when he was named Chairman of the Board in 1949.

As 3M ended 1952, its 50th anniversary year, sales were approaching $200 million, and although profit margins were very healthy, earnings had been flat since 1949. Why? To those who knew of 3M's record and took time to look more carefully, this was clearly a transitional period. New products were being developed, new plants were under construction and only one year earlier, 3M made its first direct entry into international markets. In short, 3M was poised and ready for another period of growth and had plenty of room to do so.

And grow it did! 3M's earnings progress continued uninterrupted for the next twenty-two years. A 100-share purchase of 3M stock in 1952 for $4,200 would have been valued at $109,200 at its peak twenty-one years later. Today, those same shares purchased in 1952 are enjoying an annual dividend of $3,840!

Until the company moved to St. Paul in 1910, 3M leased an old flour mill in Duluth where sandpaper was manufactured. Circa 1908.

One of the first consumer packages for 3M products: Household Wetordry water proof sandpaper.

Bing Crosby's dislike of doing "live" radio shows led to the growth of recorded commercial broadcasts and rapid expansion of "Scotch" sound recording tape, which 3M introduced in the late 1940's.

3M introduced the first presensitized offset litho plate in the 1950's.

Lewis W. Lehr, like others before him, rose "through the ranks" to become Chairman of the Board of 3M. He was closely associated with the development of 3M's health care business and is shown here (right) in pilot plant work involving packaging of surgical drapes in 1950.

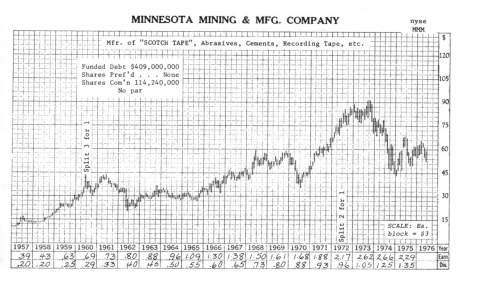

MINNESOTA MINING & MFG. COMPANY

nyse
MMM

Mfr. of "SCOTCH TAPE", Abrasives, Cements, Recording Tape, etc.

Funded Debt $409,000,000
Shares Pref'd . . . None
Shares Com'n 114,240,000
No par

Split 3 for 1

Split 2 for 1

SCALE: Ea.
block = $3

Year	1957	1958	1959	1960	1961	1962	1963	1964	1965	1966	1967	1968	1969	1970	1971	1972	1973	1974	1975	1976
Earn	39	43	.63	.69	.73	.80	.88	.96	1.09	1.30	1.38	1.50	1.61	1.68	1.88	2.17	2.62	2.66	2.29	
Div.	.20	.20	.25	.29	.33	.40	.45	.50	.55	.60	.65	.73	.80	.88	.93	.96	1.05	1.25	1.35	

Xerox Corporation

Xerox, a major manufacturer of reproduction equipment, is yet another generic term for "super stock." People are constantly talking about finding *another* Xerox in the same way King Arthur's knights must have talked about the holy grail.

Just after the turn of the century, George C. Beidler, a clerk in an abstract office in Oklahoma City, invented the Rectigraph machine for the primary purpose of developing an efficient method to copy legal documents. The resulting business, the Rectigraph Company, soon thereafter moved to Rochester, New York. In 1935, it was acquired by The Haloid Company (founded in April, 1906). For a short time, the Company was known as Haloid Xerox, Inc. and in June, 1961 was renamed Xerox Corporation.

Meanwhile, in the late 1930's, physicist Chester F. Carlson began independent experiments on photoconductors — materials that conduct electricity, especially when exposed to light. In 1940, Mr. Carlson received his first patent on a transfer electrostatic process. In the few years following, he was turned away by several companies including IBM, Eastman Kodak and RCA. In 1944, Battelle Memorial Institute agreed to further his research efforts and, three years later, The Haloid Company, in addition to its own work, began sponsoring Battelle research on the process. In 1948, after many improvements, Battelle licensed its patent rights to the process to Haloid, who, in 1950, introduced its first commercial xerographic machine — the manually-operated Model D Copier.

In the 1950's Haloid Xerox proceeded to purchase Battelle patents for cash and stock and, in an agreement effective January, 1959, acquired all improvement patents and patent applications relating to xerography owned by Battelle. Final payment under the agreement was made by Xerox in 1966 bringing the total consideration paid to $63.7 million ($9.1 million in cash and $54.6 million in stock valued at the dates of issue). In 1960, the Company introduced its first major product — the Xerox 914 which was the beginning of a revolution in office copying. For the first time, reasonably high-quality, dry copies were made automatically on ordinary paper.

Two key executives during the years of Xerox Corporation's fastest growth are pictured here with the Xerox 914, introduced in 1960. Joseph C. Wilson (right) was President from 1946 until 1966, when he was appointed Chairman of the Board. His successor as Chairman, C. Peter McColough, joined Haloid in 1954, was named Vice President-Sales in 1960, and was elected President in 1966.

In the early 1960's alone, an investment in Xerox would have doubled, then tripled, then quadrupled. In 1972, Haloid stock was selling above $170 a share compared to an adjusted cost of $1¾ in the late 1950's.

XEROX CORPORATION

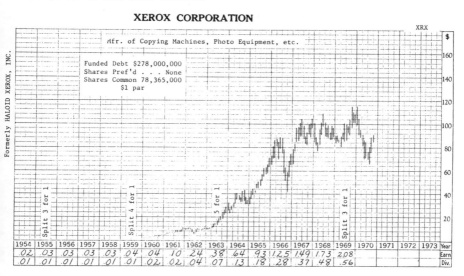

XRX

Mfr. of Copying Machines, Photo Equipment, etc.

Funded Debt $278,000,000
Shares Pref'd . . . None
Shares Common 78,365,000
$1 par

Formerly HALOID XEROX, INC.

Split 3 for 1   Split 4 for 1   Split 5 for 1   Split 3 for 1

Year	1954	1955	1956	1957	1958	1959	1960	1961	1962	1963	1964	1965	1966	1967	1968	1969	1970	1971	1972	1973
Earn	.02	.03	.03	.03	.03	.04	.04	.10	.24	.38	.64	.93	1.25	1.49	1.73	2.08				
Div.	.01	.01	.01	.01	.01	.01	.02	.02	.04	.07	.13	.18	.28	.37	.48	.56				

Walt Disney Productions

The Walt Disney experience shows that a company doesn't necessarily need technology to be a super stock.

A combination of enduring cartoon characters like Mickey Mouse and Donald Duck, a timeless film library bursting with fairytale classics like *Snow White, Cinderella* and *Pinocchio*, and the potential of its theme parks was all the magic Disney needed to become a super stock.

Until the opening of Disneyland at Anaheim, California in 1955, the company's profits were derived primarily from the production and distribution of motion picture films for theatres and television, as well as other entertainment products. In fact, ever since the company's founding in 1938, Disney's films, comic strips, book materials and licensed products have long delighted youngsters and oldsters alike.

By the early 1960's, the direction of the company's fortune was becoming clear as the Disneyland success was being translated into substantial sales and earnings gains. The opening of Disney World in Orlando, Florida in October, 1971 did

Investors who bought Disney at the high in 1970 were unhappy with the 40% + decline within six months. However, the stock was experiencing only a brief pause on its way to $496 ($124 after two 2 for 1 stock splits).

not go unnoticed by Wall Street. Its anticipation in the late 1960's and the revenue contribution that began in 1972 was not inconsequential. The stock's P/E ratio climbed from 10.7 to more than 70 times earnings between 1963 to 1973. At the same time, revenues increased from $81.9 million to $328.8 million and profits zoomed from $6.6 million to $47.8 million. Adjusted for stock splits and stock dividends, earnings advanced from 36 cents to $1.61 per share, and the value of a 100-share $4,125 investment in 1963 rose to $123,875 within ten years.

Disneyland at Anaheim, California

Walt Disney World at Orlando, Florida

Johnson & Johnson

Robert Wood Johnson and his two brothers, James Wood and Edward Mead Johnson, formed their new enterprise on the belief that "there ought to be a better way." The business, which began in 1886 on the fourth floor of a small factory building in New Brunswick, New Jersey, was incorporated as Johnson & Johnson in 1887. By 1892, the company developed a superior production method for dressings which involved a continuous dry sterilization process. Indeed, Robert Wood Johnson's idea for a new type of surgical dressing, wrapped and sealed in separate packages, and ready for immediate use, was truly a "better way."

Under the leadership of three men - Robert Wood Johnson, brother James Wood Johnson, and son General Robert Wood Johnson - the company emerged as the giant in its field.

Robert Wood Johnson joined with his two brothers to form Johnson & Johnson. He served as president between 1886 and 1910.

James Wood Johnson succeeded his brother as president in 1910 and was head of the company until 1932.

Cotton packaging at Johnson & Johnson in 1910.

General Robert Wood Johnson, son of company's first president, was an employee at Johnson & Johnson as a young man. He was, in part, responsible for the company's expansion into international markets in the early 1920's. "The General" was president from 1932 until 1963, and remained active in the company until his death in 1968.

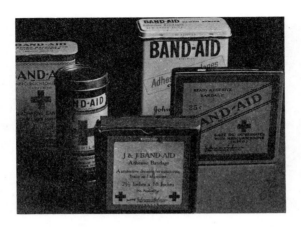

The "Band-Aid" Brand Adhesive Bandage was invented in 1920 by a Johnson & Johnson employee, Earle E. Dickson.

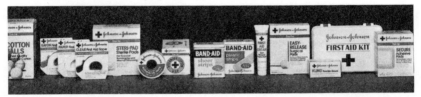

In late 1959, as the company's 72nd year was drawing to a close, an investor in Johnson & Johnson could look back a few years with a great deal of satisfaction. The stock was selling in the low 60's, triple the price of only five years earlier. After all, the company was making progress; it was the world's largest manufacturer of surgical dressings, including its well-known "Band-Aid" brand adhesive bandages. At the annual meeting, management was telling shareholders that sales were about 50% above the figures of five years ago, while, at the same time, profits climbed 55%. For 1959, Johnson & Johnson reported earnings of $1.61 per share on sales of $301 million dollars. Now, after a stock split and the addition of McNeil Laboratories, a producer of ethical drugs, acquired earlier that year, there were 5,923,000 shares outstanding. With the stock selling at nearly 40 times earnings and the prospect of slower earnings growth in 1960, might this, perhaps, be the time to sell?

A closer look at 1959, however, made this investment appear a great deal more attractive than figures in the newspapers suggested. The company's foreign profits, which were growing nicely, were not consolidated. This meant that the reported figures were somewhat understated. Moreover, promising new products were being introduced regularly, the company was very profitable with a large amount of working capital and no debt. Up to this point, the management had an outstanding record of accomplishment. Why should it not continue? Could sales not reach $600 million, or more, in the foreseeable future?

JOHNSON & JOHNSON

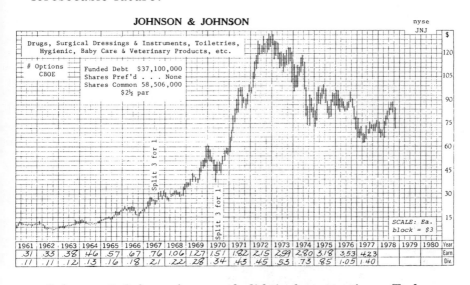

Johnson & Johnson's growth did, in fact, continue. Today, the company's sales are close to $6 billion! In 1967, and again in 1970, the stock was split 3 for 1. Johnson & Johnson stock reached a peak in 1972 of $133, an equivalent price of nearly $1,200 for that same stock held in 1959! In the perspective of the preceding twenty years, and with continuing growth still in prospect, people in 1972 had to be asking: "With the multiple at 60 times, how high is high?" And, as experienced investors today know, a little man does not come around ringing a bell, even for super stocks!

Although super stocks can pop up in any industry, many of the best performing stocks of the past have some technological orientation in their product line. Nevertheless, as Charles Allmon, head of "The Growth Stock Outlook," an investment advisory service that concentrates on small and rapidly growing companies, points out: "It isn't necessary to have a technology hardware stock to do well...nor is it desirable in relationship to risk. You can buy value and be safe and secure in knowing that that value will eventually be reflected in the market price."

All true and all to the good. But a review of the best performers does suggest that technology, more than not, is a better bet.

Texas Instruments has been on the leading edge of technology for nearly three decades. The company introduced the first integrated circuit in 1958, with much credit going to scientist Jack Kilby. In the late 1950's, Texas Instruments' stock soared more than 4,700%!

In addition to size and a leaning toward technology, the better performing stocks seem to possess a majority of the following characteristics:

- A leading position in an attractive industry.
- A proprietary product or service that will do an essential job better or cheaper than the competition.
- Strong, progressive, and research-minded management.
- An ability to develop new products and penetrate new markets.
- Rising sales accompanied by continuing growth in unit demand.
- A healthy return on stockholders' equity, with improvement over the years.
- A relatively low labor cost.
- The means to finance future growth internally with minimal reliance on capital markets.
- An ability to produce high profit margins on sales with the immediate prospect of rising profit margins.
- The ability to raise prices as costs go up, without attracting political opposition.
- A strong financial position (low debt).
- A high plowback ratio of earnings.
- Conservative, sensible accounting.
- A limited exposure to environmental, social, political pressures.
- Reasonable freedom from import competition.
- Rising earnings per share relative to most other stocks.
- The stock should not yet be too popular among the institutions.
- Rising dividends, although the payout ratio (amount of dividends paid out of earnings) should be fairly low to allow for a generous plowback of earnings.
- A stable or rising price earnings multiple.

Each of these 19 characteristics has something going for it. And each, by itself, at the right time and in the right market, can move a stock's price up. But a careful examination of the "super stock" successes in all the market periods described thus far gradually eliminates characteristic after characteristic. Not every super stock on the list had conservative, sensible accounting. Nor did each of our winners have top-notch proprietary products, services or skills. As a matter of fact, careful examination of all super stocks eliminated all but nine characteristics that were common to all super stocks. None had less than these nine! They were:

1. Small to medium size.
2. Rising unit sales volume.
3. Rising pretax profit margins.
4. Above-average, and improving, return on stockholders' equity.
5. Strong earnings per share growth relative to most stocks.
6. A low payout ratio with rising dividends.
7. Low debt ratio.
8. Low institutional holdings.
9. Increasing price earnings multiple.

Each of these nine characteristics — so important to our search for the "super stock" — will now be described in detail.

Out Of The Forest, Into The Trees

Size of the Company

Most super stocks experience a point where management is reasonably well seasoned and, at the same time, the company has reached a good size (that is, a sales volume large enough to be generating a useful cash flow of meaningful proportions). Moreover, the company, or the market it is serving, is usually not yet quite large enough to attract major competition. At such a point, the company is hungry — hungry for people, for more working space, and for new ideas. The company is simply hungry for new worlds to conquer.

Accordingly, we are seeking businesses that are on the "threshold" of fast growth. These are companies with annual sales of $25 million to $500 million, depending on the industry. Companies this size are in the most volatile segment of the corporate spectrum since it is especially demanding of managerial skills.

These threshold companies are extremely explosive and can spurt ahead by finding and exploiting a market niche too small or specialized to attract billion-dollar enterprises. But the risk is also great. Typically, the company is more vulnerable to industry downturns due to less diversification, more in need on costly debt financing, and shorter on staying power in a recession. These companies must evolve as they grow. A small company can remain under its founder's close supervision and still prosper by offering a single line of relatively simple products sold over a limited geographic area to a smaller number of customers. By contrast, with growth, there are also difficult management problems such as delegation of authority, as well as a need for planning and market research. All require new layers of management. And that is "another world" to many entrepreneurs.

Each economic shake-out sees a number of these companies fail completely or merge with unfavorable terms just to survive. But others continue to grow at high rates, even in a difficult economic environment. One important factor for survival and growth rate continuation is maintaining profit margins in an economic downturn. These successful companies can, and usually do, react quickly by raising prices to pass along costs and by weeding out less profitable items. They also display "the entrepreneurial courage" to get full price for what they sell. They search out items that are less sensitive to price competition and focus their attention on these items.

Additionally, the successful "threshold companies" also stay close to their market niches. Diversification spreads the risk but also dilutes profitability. Rather than overextending themselves or risking a head-on collision with more powerful competitors, the successful company concentrates on market segments that huge corporations often ignore.

Finally, a threshold company's chief executive officer is often a critical element. Unlike a giant corporation, where the chief executive is usually bolstered by stable echelons of trained managers, a smaller company — for better or worse — is greatly shaped by its top man or woman. Much depends on that executive's ability to adapt himself and the company to the changing demands of growth. But overall, the most important task is to sustain top management's drive and to maintain the company's vitality as long as possible.

Size, then, is one of the critical characteristics of our super stock. . .not too big. . .not too small. We want a threshold company with sales and earnings ready to accelerate.

This specific size range also tends to minimize our risk since we are not investing in newly born companies. We have seen the company prove itself in the real world for a few years. This means, of course, that we have also given up some of the initial gain enjoyed by the founders of the company. That's fine. They've earned it by taking the biggest risk. But even bigger gains are about to occur if we're right about the company and the stock. Explosive sales and earnings growth will result in significantly higher stock prices once investors begin to recognize the potential of our super stock.

How do we identify both the company and its "threshold point"?

Recall the corporate life cycle discussed earlier. At the take-off stage when the value of the company's services or products are perceived in the marketplace, sales begin to increase dramatically. Earnings will tend to increase even faster as the power of sales leverage begins to display itself. This is the ideal point to buy the stock. Sales and earnings over the past several years have demonstrated the company's viability. The company is no longer completely vulnerable and mistakes in investment timing can be absorbed more readily. While the initial stock investors (including venture capitalists) have probably doubled or tripled their money, there is still plenty of capital appreciation left if the company continues its course. Furthermore, although the investment risk is quite high, there is substantially less risk than one, two, or a few years before. This stage also represents the period in which shrewd investors are beginning to analyze the stock and a few institutions have begun to invest.

The sharp curving climb to stage 4 (maturity) constitutes the period of maximum gain. In stage 4, age is setting in and the growth will taper. This is also the period when the major institutions have already become or are becoming stockholders. Newspapers will call it a "glamour" stock while others may call it a "Blue Chip." No matter what the name, growth in the stock price will probably continue, but at a slower pace. Note, too, that these "super stock" phases may last long periods of time. . .totaling five, ten or fifteen years. At stage 3, the future appears bright and the company's earnings potential seems unlimited. By looking for stocks of "threshold" companies, we are inventorying them before the majority of institutions recognize their potential. At some point, when institutional investors finally begin to buy our super stock, we, as investors with long term perspective, will gladly enjoy the ride.

Unit Sales Volume

Rising sales volume is essential to any growth company. (Here, the term "sales" refers to net sales — the actual sales and/or revenues after deducting allowances, returns and cash discounts taken by customers. However, this is usually not a critical distinction.) How fast should sales be rising? As a general rule, growth should not be less than an annual rate of 12-15% during a strong economic year. Furthermore, the prospects of 15-20% (or more) annually should not be out of reach.

On the other hand, a rising sales trend does not always mean a company is enjoying greater prosperity. Sales may be going up, but overall expenses to produce those products or services may be going up even faster. It is possible for a company to survive this squeeze temporarily by cutting expenses or by producing more with the same, or less, labor and equipment. But without sales growth, in today's environment, a company is ultimately doomed. Not only are rising sales essential to corporate profits, they are also a thermometer of corporate health. A rising sales trend means the company's products and services are winning greater acceptance with the customer and that the company's marketing efforts are successful.

There is, however, a "catch" when using rising sales volume as a sought-after characteristic of a super stock. The best way to describe this "trap" is to offer an example. Let's look at XYZ Corporation's record of increasing sales:

XYZ CORPORATION

Net Sales in $ 000's

	Year 1	Year 2	Year 3	Year 4	Year 5
Reported Net Sales	$10,000	$12,000	$15,000	$17,000	$20,000
% Change	—	+ 20%	+ 25%	+ 13%	+ 18%

A pretty good sales record. Right? Net sales doubled in four years. That's an annual growth rate of nearly 20%! But remember, the sales figure also includes prices. We should look at these sales figures and compare them to the actual unit volume of products shipped. In this case, if the company sold 1 million units at $10 each in the first year, and 10% more, or 1,100,000 units in the second year, but dollar sales volume increased 20%, why the difference? Answer: an increase in prices. This could be a reflection of rising costs in an inflationary period. If it happens again in the third, fourth and fifth years, dollar sales will continue to rise faster than unit volume. And, frequently, price increases will adversely impact unit growth, or perhaps hide a slowdown that might already be occurring in unit sales. It is possible that, despite a reported increase in sales, XYZ Corporation has lost momentum in the marketing of its products or services. This could be an early danger sign of a weakening competitive situation. Had the XYZ Corporation reported the sales and unit volume figures shown below, the conclusion might be less favorable:

XYZ CORPORATION

	Year 1	Year 2	Year 3	Year 4	Year 5
Reported Net Sales	$10,000	$12,000	$15,000	$17,000	$20,000
% Change	—	+ 20%	+ 25%	+ 13%	+ 18%
Unit Sales Volume	1,000	1,100	1,200	1,250	1,225
% Change	—	+ 10%	+ 9%	+ 4%	− 2%
Unit Price	$10.00	$10.91	$12.50	$13.60	$16.33
% Price Change	—	+ 9.1%	+ 14.6%	+ 8.8%	+ 20.1%

The point is that unit sales growth is one of the most important characteristics separating the ordinary growth company from the super stock. Sales volume in dollars is a good initial indicator, but a strong showing in unit growth is more conclusive.

Without knowing a company's unit shipments, there is an easy, shortcut way to measure unit growth. By adjusting the company's reported dollar sales figures by the overall inflation rate of the economy (i.e., using the annual percentage change of the Consumer Price Index — see Appendix "A"), an investor can make an "educated guess" of unit growth. If, for example, reported dollar sales advanced 19% and CPI increased 8% that year, the unit growth would be approximately 11%. This is, admittedly, a rough calculation. And, without care, it could be misleading. However, short of obtaining figures directly from the company, this approach is the most effective method.

One further note of caution when analyzing large companies with extensive overseas operations: Sales can be greatly influenced by changes in international currency rates. Adjustments can be made quite easily using the figures usually found in the footnotes of the annual reports. However, for most "threshold" companies, international sales are still only a small, growing part of the business (and, in fact, just one more reason for substantial growth in the years ahead).

Rising Profit Margin

A company's profit margin can be defined as the relationship of income (profit) before, or after, taxes to net sales. If a company, Alpha Corporation, had net sales of $35.6 million and if the total expense of generating those sales (production costs plus selling, administrative costs, etc.) was $28.7 million, then the company's profit before taxes would be $6.9 million. This would be a pretax profit margin of 19.5% ($6.9 million divided by $35.6 million). The pretax margin reflects the efficiency of a company to extract a profit from each dollar of sales. Also, more than any other ratio or percentage, the pretax profit margin indiates just how profitable and effective a company has been within its industry. Most experts favor pretax profit margins as an analytical tool since the profitability of one company can be compared against another without the variables of different tax rates.

As a general rule, very few super stocks have pretax profit margins below 10-12%. Once in the growth phase, a 15-20% (or more) margin is not unusual. For example, Alpha Corporation presented their income statement as follows:

ALPHA CORPORATION

Income Statement

	Year Ended December 31	
	Last Year	Year Before
Net Sales	$35,598,782	$30,945,236
Cost of Goods Sold	20,009,100	17,289,604
Gross Profit	$15,589,682	$13,655,632
Selling, Admin. & Gen'l. Expenses	9,370,600	8,678,577
Operating Profit	$ 6,219,082	$ 4,977,055
Profit Before Taxes	$ 6,954,136	$ 5,739,901
Pretax Profit Margin	19.5%	18.5%
Provision for Taxes	2,791,230	2,548,090
Net Profit	$ 4,162,906	$ 3,225,811

In this case, Alpha's pretax profit margin increased from 18.5% to 19.5% in the most recent year.

Put another way — if Alpha Corporation makes 19½¢ for every $1.00 of sales, we know that Alpha's management is doing a better job than the competition who might only being doing, say, 12%.

Profit margins tell us more eloquently than words that one company is operating much more efficiently than another. It is an affirmation of a company's skill in controlling the costs of doing business. The fact that Alpha's cost of goods sold is now proportionately higher than it was earlier is a point of concern and bears watching. But, overall, the company's profitability improved.

Not only are Alpha's sales rising, but management is also more skillful in capturing profits. Now we can compare Alpha to other companies in the industry and to the industry average each year to be sure Alpha is maintaining its profitability. If profit margins were drifting down rather than advancing, we might monitor the company's progress, hoping to spot the turnaround margins. Declining profit margins could be a temporary situation — the economy, perhaps, or unusual operating expenses related to a new, more efficient plant, or the startup of a new operation. Any of these could restore or enhance profit margins. If one of these is the explanation, fine. We'll watch and wait for the beginning of the turn and defer buying the stock until there are definite signs of improvement. Sometimes getting a new plant up to speed takes longer than expected. So, we carefully plot the company's progress quarter-by-quarter to detect the beginning of the turnaround in margins. However, if we bought the stock on rising profit margins and then, suddenly, they declined, we would consider this to be a danger signal. The question then would be: Is this temporary? Do we have an unusual situation because of expansion, or a bad economy, or has management lost control of expenses? We may have misjudged the company. Is competition getting keener, requiring price cutting and heavier marketing expenses?

High pretax profit margins (above 10-15%) are desirable because they give a corporation the profits for further growth. But more important than the magnitude of the margins is the *trend* extending over several years. The trend must be level or rising. It should never be falling, unless from extremely high, unsustainable levels.

Earlier, it was noted that the profit margin is the relationship of income to net sales. But this takes into account only two of the three essential factors in a corporation meeting its profit objective: sales and expenses. The third is investment. A new plant increase of capacity by 20% requires substantial investment to achieve this 20% increase in sales. If profit margins were the only basis of measurement, many multi-product companies would give emphasis to product lines with high margins, but with low return on investment, rather than to those lines with high return on investment. As a result, reliance on the profit margin computation as a sole measurement for calculating profitability is misplaced.

The profit margin tells us how much profit is realized from sales, but doesn't take into account the amount of investment required to produce those sales. Since investment in plant and equipment ultimately produces sales, we want to know how efficient a company is in utilizing invested funds. This brings us to the most important criterion: Rate of Return on Stockholders' Equity.

Return on Stockholders' Equity

Just as the profit margin percentage is a measure of management's efficiency in extracting profits from each sales dollar, the profit earned on the stockholders' investment is the indicator of management's efficiency in using the stockholders' funds remaining in the company. In other words, what has been management's productivity of capital?

The best way to measure "productivity of capital" is to track the profitability of the company's "Stockholders' Equity" (total assets less total liabilities), sometimes also called "Net Worth," by relating the company's profit to the level of stockholders' equity. In so doing, we can see just how successful management has been with the stockholders' money. This calculation is referred to as "Return on Stockholders' Equity," or simply, "Return on Equity." It is found in the following manner:

$$\frac{\text{Net profit after taxes}}{\text{Stockholders' Equity}} = \text{\% Return on Stockholders' Equity}$$

If the company has preferred stock, the return on equity is calculated by first deducting the preferred stock dividend from the net profit, and deducting the par value of the preferred stock from the stockholders' equity before dividing.

Furthermore, to be precise, when figuring return on equity, it is better to average the year-beginning and year-ending stockholders' equity rather than just using the year-end figure in the calculation. The net income was earned over an entire twelve-month period. Therefore, it should be related to the *average* stockholders' equity rather than just the year-end figure. However, for the sake of simplicity and speed, the year-end stockholders' equity figure does suffice for a rough calculation.

If the principal goal of our target company is increasing profit, the purpose of retaining the profit is to enjoy a reasonable percentage return on the money management is investing for us. Otherwise, it should be paid out as dividends. Further, management has a responsibility to earn on the stockholders' capital *at least* that amount available on alternative investments. If the company cannot earn a *reasonable* return for investors, then they should be able to recover their money and put it to more productive uses themselves. They should ask management to forsake growth and return their investment as dividends.

But it is a rare corporate situation where the stockholders can jointly put such a question to management and receive a response. Typically, management will seek other avenues of growth, new areas of expansion or acquisitions rather than confess their inability to earn a market rate of return. The historical returns for many listed companies, particularly in the steel industry, are woefully below market returns over long periods of time. These companies have persisted in pouring cash into low-return businesses for years, hoping for better times. They would have done better either paying out the cash to investors in the form of higher dividends or simply investing the money in Treasury Bills. In either case, the stockholder would have been better off. *But* you don't retain high-priced management to invest in Treasury Bills. So management continues to throw good money after bad. The result is usually disastrous for shareholders.

		RETURN ON STOCKHOLDERS' EQUITY		
Years	Steel Co. A	Steel Co. B	Steel Co. C	Average Interest on Treasury Bills
1	4.3%	—	4.5%	5.0%
2	4.3	4.2%	6.6	5.0
3	8.2	8.2	6.1	7.1
4	15.1	15.4	8.7	8.2
5	11.5	5.9	13.4	6.9
6	8.0	4.9	9.1	6.0
7	2.7	3.0	6.9	6.0
8	4.6	8.4	—	8.2
9	—	8.6	9.1	10.5
10	9.5	3.4	4.7	12.3

If you, as a stockholder, cannot convince management to return part of your accumulated profits or to invest in more favorable investment areas, take your money and run. You sell your stock and move elsewhere.

Each year, numerous statistical services and business magazines will release annual reviews and surveys of sales, profits and other figures, including returns on equity. One such survey conducted recently provided figures (which will change from one year to the next) for several selected industries. The table appears on page 144.

Given the wide variety of returns, what constitutes an above-average return? There is no single answer, but in our super stock search we are looking for a company whose return is: (1) Better than the competition; (2) Above the aggregate rates of return of the companies in broad market averages such as the S&P and the Dow Industrials; and (3) Above the prevailing level of interest rates. For the sake of this discussion, it can be said that any return on equity below 15% is not satisfactory. Moreover, like pretax margins, the *trend* is important. As the company gains maturity, its productivity improves and its assets are used to greater advantage.

Above-average returns fuel the ram-jet engine of growth. If a company earns 20% on stockholders' equity and pays out half in dividends, the remaining 50% will be plowed back into the business to produce a future growth rate of roughly 10% (20% X 50%). And if the company pays out only 15% of earnings as dividends, the remaining 85%, given a 20% rate of return on stockholders' equity, will sustain a growth rate of about 17% (20% X 85%)! In light of these calculations, a natural question becomes: Why doesn't management keep every last penny of earnings, paying out nothing? The answer to this question is considered later in the section: *Low, But Rising Dividends.*

Relative Earnings Per Share Growth

Earnings can be increased in several ways: through cost reductions while sales remain relatively stable, thus improving profit margins; by increasing sales and maintaining the same profit margins; or, in the ideal situation, by increasing sales and increasing profit margins at the same time. Accordingly, a super stock is one that increases its sales at a fast clip while improving margins. But note that increased sales is a usual requirement for significant earnings growth. And note also that while total earnings are important, earnings per share is the key element watched by investors.

Any study of high performance stocks reveals that their earnings increased at a compound annual rate in excess of both the Dow and the S&P. Stock prices react immediately to any significant change in either current earnings or short-term earnings prospects. In a sense, we're trying to buy *growing* earnings as cheaply as possible. This is related to three factors: the rate of future earnings growth of the company; the degree of certainty that this growth will occur; and, the price earnings multiple.

Not all earnings are the same. A dollar of earnings by one company can be valued differently by investors than that same dollar generated by another company. The dependability of earnings could be one factor. The state of the economy and monetary conditions (particularly interest rates) could be another. They all affect investor psychology and thus the price earnings multiple. For example, the Dow Jones Industrial Average once sold at 23 times the earnings of its component stocks (in 1961) but it has also sold at 6 or 7 times those earnings in other years.

A good example of this phenomenon occurred in the heyday of growth stocks between 1960 and 1972. At this time, there was a mania among institutional investors for growing and predictable earnings. It was the period of what many called "the two-tiered market."

Mr. V.T. Norton, then Chairman of the Board of the Amerace Corporation, gave a dramatic example of the two-tiered market where large institutions were buying stocks of the *favorite fifty.* As the theory goes, they have superior growth in both earnings and dividends which entitles them to high multiples.

Mr. Norton was in disagreement. According to him, "A substantial portion of these high multiples is caused by what has been labeled an 'inadvertent conspiracy' created when the institutions get on and ride. Having taken major positions for themselves or their clients, their continued recommendations or purchases of these stocks may well be in fact a conflict of interest."

Mr. Norton added that no one would "quarrel" with the premise that good continuous earnings should be attractive to investors. "Some companies," he said, "should enjoy higher price-earnings multiples than others. However, this does not justify the stratospheric multiples in the stocks that are the darlings of the money managers."

Mr. Norton then pointed out the earnings record of his company, Amerace, compared with one of the premier growth stocks of the period. . .one of the most favored of the favorite fifty:

Year	Amerace	Avon
1968	$2.00	$1.24
1969	1.77	1.47
1970	1.81	1.72
1971	2.14	2.16
Total share earnings (five years)	$9.69	$8.48
Dividends (five years)	$6.00	$5.38

It is clear that Amerace earned more money per share than Avon during the period. The problem, of course, was that Amerace's earnings were neither growing nor consistent. The break in 1969 earnings posed a major question of continuity. The premium then, as now, was on consistency of earnings growth. At the time of Mr. Norton's comments, his company,

Amerace, was selling at a price earnings ratio of 6 and Avon was selling at 50! Was Avon worth such a premium for consistency? In hindsight, the answer was no. Avon's stock later went from its multiple of 50 to a single digit multiple when earnings declined and investor psychology turned sour.

What determines price earnings multiples is the expected future rate of growth of a company's earnings and the stability of these future earnings. Once this stability (or persistency) has been established, the price that investors are willing to pay for that certainty goes up, as it did with Avon. But woe unto the company that, after compiling an excellent long term growth rate, suddenly suffers a break in earnings. This, of course, is what happened in the case of Avon and many others in the early 1970's.

Not too many years ago, a fairly exhaustive study was conducted to determine the answer to the question: What is the major factor that will determine the performance of a company's stock in the future (over the next two to three years). The approach involved gathering a universe of companies with similar fundamental and technical characteristics. This group consisted of all companies from 1966 to 1973 that showed each of the following three characteristics on April 30th of 1973:

    (a) a Price/Earnings Ratio of 40 or greater;

    (b) a market value of $100 million or higher;

    (c) most recently reported earnings at a maximum level for the prior five years.

There were 116 companies with these characteristics including such companies as Avon, Baxter Labs, Corning Glass, Eastman Kodak, Johnson & Johnson, Eli Lilly, and so on. The second step was to note the earnings and price performance of these companies over the 3 years following.

Eighty-six of the 116 companies showed an earnings increased over the next 3 years while only 30 showed an earnings decrease. The average price change of these 116 companies over the subsequent 3 years was +7%. Thus, over this period, these companies performed about in line with the market.

The major result, however, was that the 86 companies showing an earnings increase during this period actually performed very well indeed. They enjoyed an average price appreciation of 42%. About 3 out of 4 of these companies actually showed a rise in price, whereas only 1 out of 4 showed a decline.

The companies that showed an earnings decrease registered an average price decline of 60%. Only 1 out of 30 companies showing an earnings decline managed to show a price advance. Companies showing an earnings increase showed price appreciation more than 100% better than the companies showing an earnings decrease.

Eight of the ten companies that showed the largest earnings increase during this period went up in price and their average gain was 60.3%. The ten companies that showed the worst earnings performance declined an average of 58.4% in just three years. The latter group also included two companies that fell into bankruptcy. In summary, this study indicated that the one factor that determined the price appreciation of all the large growth companies in this review was *earnings increases.*

Finally, the New York Stock Exchange monitors the high earnings performers among its listed companies. In the past 23 years in which statistics have been compiled on listed companies, only twelve have consistently, year in and year out, increased sales, net income and earnings per share. The next two tables present that select group arrayed two ways; first, size; and then earnings per share growth.

Company	1980 SALES (in millions)
1. Procter & Gamble	$10,772
2. Beatrice Foods	8,772
3. Philip Morris, Inc.	7,328
4. American Home Products	3,798
5. Bristol-Myers	3,158
6. Kellogg Co.	2,150
7. Petrolane, Inc.	1,425
8. Chesebrough-Ponds	1,377
9. Baxter Travenol Labs	1,374
10. Deluxe Check Printers	428
11. NCH	322
12. Jostens	295

Company	Earnings Per Share Growth 23-Yr. Annual Compound Rate
1. Baxter Travenol Labs	20.0%
2. NCH	18.6%
3. Deluxe Check Printers	17.3%
4. Petrolane, Inc.	17.2%
5. Jostens	16.1%
6. Philip Morris, Inc.	15.0%
7. Bristol-Myers	14.7%
8. Chesebrough-Ponds	12.6%
9. Kellogg Co.	10.5%
10. American Home Products	10.4%
11. Procter & Gamble	10.4%
12. Beatrice Foods	9.3%

Can you guess which of these companies had the best stock performance in the same period? You guessed it! Baxter's stock rose by a fantastic 8,220%!

With this background, then, it's easy to see why "relative earnings growth" is an important factor in our search for the next super stock. One fast and easy way to make this calculation is to compare the earnings per share growth of our super stock candidates to the earnings growth of the "market" over some recent timeframe. Since one year is a fairly short period of time, and much can happen to a small, rapidly growing company in five years, three years was selected for this study. Simply calculate the growth of earnings per share over the past three years. Then, compare it to the growth of the Dow Industrial's earnings (see Appendix "B") over the same period. Thus, we have a means of judging relative earnings growth.

Low, But Rising Dividends

Dividends are clinically explained as the proportion of net earnings paid out to stockholders by a corporation. The dividend payment by a corporation is statistically portrayed in two ways: dividend yield and dividend payout. Like the price earnings ratio, dividend statistics are an important indicator of a company's value in the marketplace and its future growth. Dividend yield is expressed as a percentage calculated by dividing the current annual dividend by the market price of the stock. Since the price of a stock changes from day to day, so does the yield. Yields are calculated daily for listed stocks in the stock tables of most major newspapers. Yields on over-the-counter stocks appear on a weekly basis in financial weeklies such as *Barron's*. The percentage of the company's earnings paid out in dividends to the stockholders is called the dividend payout ratio. If a company earns $1.00 per share and pays out $0.10 per share, the payout ratio is 10%.

A company with growing earnings has two choices: it can pay the earnings out in dividends or it can keep the money in the company, plowing it back into the business to earn even more money. Both dividends and retained earnings have already been taxed once, but dividends will be taxed again once distributed to the shareholder. Retained earnings, on the other hand, can be reinvested in the business tax-free. If management is doing its job, it should be able to earn a greater return for shareholders than they can earn left to their own devices.

The dividend payout ratio is important because of the taxes on dividends and the tax-free nature of the plowback in earnings. If invested properly, this plowback increases earnings power, and eventually the price of the stock. Thus, we have a long-term capital gains potential. Long-term capital gains (assets held more than one year) are subject to taxation only upon sale of the appreciated asset and at rates less than at income tax rates. As a result, for most investors, after-tax dividend dollars are worth less than capital gains dollars. It also means that low-dividend-payout stocks of rapid-growth businesses are more attractive to investors in high tax brackets.

Interestingly, there is a prevailing view that a high payout gives the investor some protection in the event of a market decline. At some point in a stock's decline, the theory goes, the yield on a stock will be so high that the stock will be cushioned from going down any further. Unfortunately, this theory ignores the fact that concern over the future viability of earnings is one of the main reasons a stock declines in the first place. And once the future earnings stream comes into question, investors will usually give little credit to the current dividend. They realize if earnings fall, the dividend will soon follow and there goes the yield. There is, therefore, one rule worth noting: "If you have a choice between buying a stock that yields 2% and one that yields 7%, and have absolutely no other information at all about the two stocks, you can, without hesitation, select the stock yielding 2%. Nine times out of ten it will turn out to be the better investment of the two."

So, in general, low dividend payouts are better than high dividend payouts. And, if this is true, then no payout must be even better. Right? Logical, but incorrect as far as the stock market is concerned. For one thing, a great many institutions will not place a stock on their "buy" list unless it pays a dividend. A dividend makes the stock a true investment. Moreover, as the discussion in Chapter IV demonstrated, dividends play an important role in an investor's portfolio.

Also important is the fact that a dividend, particularly a dividend rising over time, is often a "signal" from management to the investing public. Generally, changes in stock prices come about by changes in investor expectation about future earnings. Dividend increases indicate management's confidence that earnings increases will be forthcoming. That's a signal investors like because managements are usually extremely reluctant to increase dividends unless they're certain of future earnings gains.

Dividend decisions are based on management's desire to establish a pattern of stable dividend growth. A reluctance to change prevails both in regard to dividend increases and decreases. Increases in dividends are slow in coming because it indicates a commitment to continue paying at that level. A number of studies, some based on interviews with corporate management, and others that have reviewed dividend histories, reaffirm the point that companies do not make dividend changes without considerable reflection about the future. Reductions usually occur only when companies have no other choice. Therefore, dividend changes reflect management's opinion about the future and should serve as indicators of a firm's future prosperity.

Clearly, from the investor's standpoint, the ideal dividend is a realistic balance between the company's needs for future growth and the investor's reward for patience.

What is the right balance? There is no definite answer, but consider the following table:

Potential Annual Growth Rate (Reinvestment Rate)

RETURN ON EQUITY	PAYOUT 0	10%	20%	30%	40%	50%
10%	10%	9%	8%	7%	6%	5%
15%	15%	14%	12%	11%	9%	8%
20%	20%	18%	16%	14%	12%	10%
25%	25%	23%	20%	18%	15%	13%
30%	30%	27%	24%	21%	18%	15%
35%	35%	32%	28%	25%	21%	18%
40%	40%	36%	32%	28%	24%	20%

Source: Based on the Reinvestment Rate formula as described in Understanding Wall Street, *1982. (Liberty Publishing Company, Inc.)*

The table illustrates, for example, that if a company has a return on average stockholders' equity of 20% and a payout ratio of 30% (ie., a plowback of 70%), the investor can expect an annual earnings growth rate of approximately 14%. The higher the ROE, the more a company can afford to pay in dividends without affecting earnings growth. If our super stock candidate has little hope for a return on equity of much more 15%, a payout ratio of 40% is high enough!

Low Debt Ratio

Many investors swear they'll only invest in companies with "clean" balance sheets; that is, no debt. Unfortunately, these investors could be missing some good opportunities because debt, used properly, can increase earnings dramatically. Take the case of a corporation in the 1960's that sold bonds at a 5% interest rate. That's cheap capital today, and since interest costs are deductible, the after-tax cost to the company is even less. Using debt to increase earnings is called "leveraging," and many companies have been successful using this technique.

"The problem with debt is that it has to be paid off—usually at the most inconvenient time for a corporation..." The speaker was one of the founding DuPonts in a letter to a friend. This comment reflects DuPont Company's problem with debt in its formative years and explains the company's aversion to debt, at least until recent times.

An old rule of thumb says that debt is dangerous for cyclical companies, such as the steels and autos. In these cases, it was said, preferred stock should be substituted and then a payment (the dividend) can be missed without financial disaster. This point ignores the obvious additional expense for safety: interest payments are deductible for tax purposes; preferred dividends are not. Where a corporation has a 50% effective tax rate, the cost of preferred financing, then, is twice that of bonds. Is safety worth the additional cost?

With leveraging, wide changes in earnings may be expected because debt interest payments and/or preferred dividend payments must be absorbed before anything is left for common stockholders. It works to the advantage of shareholders when earnings are good. It works against them when earnings are bad. Take the case of leverage at work with ABC Company. Over an economic cycle comprising a five-year period, sales go up steadily through the first three years. Profit margins are maintained as sales increase, allowing earnings, before interest, to benefit directly from the increased revenues. Indeed, earnings rise dramatically from $0.24 a share to $0.39. But as the recession hits in the fourth year, the decline is dramatic.

	—Years—				
	1	**2**	**3**	**4**	**5**
Earnings Before Interest	$580,000	$720,000	$870,000	$280,000	$ 30,000
Interest Expense	100,000	100,000	100,000	100,000	100,000
Earnings Before Income Taxes	480,000	620,000	770,000	180,000	(70,000)
Income Taxes (@ 50%)	240,000	320,000	385,000	90,000	—
Net Earnings	240,000	320,000	385,000	90,000	(70,000)
Net Earnings Per Share	.24	.32	.39	.09	(.07)

The wide swing in earnings is accentuated by the subtraction of the fixed amount of interest expense. In other words, the excess of the rate earned on investment over the rate paid for borrowed money is the degree of leverage. In this example, the fifth year is critical; total earnings are not enough to cover the interest payments and ABC Company has to dip into reserves to pay the interest. If there are no reserves to make the interest payments, or if the debt is close to maturity, the company could be in deep trouble...financial insolvency at worst, and financial embarrassment at best. Leverage, then, works both ways. It magnifies the good times and bad times alike. Accordingly, a shift in the company's cost structure toward more fixed costs of any type (debt, of course, is not the only kind) tends to increase the magnitude of investment risk.

Given the dangers of too much debt, is there a rule that investors can follow? The answer depends on the industry and stability of earning power, the company's profitability (especially measured by the return on shareholders' equity), and, of course, the level of interest rates (a 20% interest rate can be a much greater drain on the company's resources than, say, a rate of 4%). For utilities, where the markets are monopolistic with only one company in the area, a debt level of 50% or 60% of the total capitalization is not out of line. For cyclical companies such as steel, aluminum, and copper companies, debt percentages above 25% of total capitalization should be viewed very carefully. With growth companies, we can be somewhat more liberal. Our rule should be that debt will not exceed 35% of the total capitalization. This means that, roughly, debt should not be more than 50% of stockholders' equity...especially if the return on stockholders' equity is less than 20%. When interest rates are high, the lower the debt, the better.

Could this company be in trouble? Management appears optimistic. The company declared a cash dividend for the first time in nearly twenty years and the stock is listed on the New York Stock Exchange.

Year	Sales ($mm)	— Per Share — Earnings	Dividend
1980	$709.6	$0.76	$0.10
1979	648.8	0.92	—
1978	575.6	0.94	—
1977	511.5	0.59	—
1976	474.7	0.53	—

— 1980 Capitalization —

Debt	$210.0 million
Equity	127.8 million

7,100,000 shares outstanding

That's right! This company, Saxon Industries, declared bankruptcy in 1982. A quick glance at the figures, of course, tells the investor that Saxon was never close to being a super stock (note, for example, the low profit margins and the poor return on stockholders' equity). However, this example does show what can happen when debt is too high, even though sales are increasing and the company is profitable.

Institutional Holdings

Investors are always surprised when they discover a company that has earnings per share growth well above average over a considerable period of time and yet its stock has not advanced substantially in price. Suspiciously, they begin to believe something must be wrong. And yet further checking produces no flaws: unit sales volume up, pretax profit margins up, the return on equity up — all the characteristics of a super stock exist, and still the price has failed to keep pace with these achievements. The primary reason, of course, is *size*. The company is simply too small for institutions to buy the stock in a big way.

Most big institutions are interested only in companies with capitalizations above $200 million and only a few will buy when a capitalization is much under $50 million. This is where the flexibility and patience of the individual investor can become a substantial advantage.

You can find the institutional ownership of most companies in Vickers or from Moody's or Standard & Poor's. The Standard & Poor's monthly stock guide, for example, lists more than 5100 common and preferred stocks with some operating history, financial statistics, etc. One of the columns lists the number of institutions holding the stock and the number of shares owned. The data covers almost 2550 institutions including investment companies, banks, insurance companies, college endowments and so on.

We want our stock to be relatively unknown — but not completely. Some modest institutional ownership is comforting. Institutions spend a lot of time and money researching a stock. Their research is intensive and thorough and most investors know it. So, having a few institutions own the stock represents respectability and a vindication of our research process. It also suggests that other investors with more sophisticated tools and resources independently agree regarding our target company's growth and prospect. It's almost a badge of acceptance. But just as with dividends, a little ownership is fine, but not too much.

The company is still to be "discovered" when institutional ownership is below 10%. Usually, by the time holdings exceed 15%, the stock is on the "approved lists" of a large number of institutions. Dave Baker, one of the most successful and respected portfolio managers on Wall Street once said: "When all the institutions are in. . .there's no one else with big buying power to put the stock price up further. Success is only greeted with a yawn. . .it's expected. But failure. . .a bad quarter. . .and all the institutions will want to go out of the door at once. It can make for a very volatile stock. . .and a disappointing one."

In two or three years, perhaps less, our super stock's high rate of growth in sales and earnings will begin to place it on the edge of consideration among the smaller institutions. They will begin to buy and put the price up. The company's rapid growth will raise earnings per share and, with it, increased institutional acceptance will expand the multiple. Since capitalization requirements of an institution is a function of both shares outstanding and price, growth in earnings, coupled with the higher multiple, will ultimately place our selected stock within the universe of most institutions. And institutions will be important in our stock's future; for it is *they who will contribute much of that second ingredient to our "Magic Combination," thus making it a "super" stock.*

Price Earnings Multiple

A basic tool in valuing earnings is the price earnings multiple, or P/E ratio. This indicates what the stock market is willing to pay for a dollar of earnings. Price earnings multiples are important since appreciation in a growth stock is achieved not only by the steadily increasing per-share earnings, but also through a rising P/E ratio. This point is best shown by this example of an 8-year price appreciation of American Home Products Corporation from 1953 through 1961:

Year	Sales	Earnings Per Share	Year End Market Price	P/E Ratio
1961	$468.2 mm	$2.16	$78	36.1x
1960	446.5	2.09	60	28.7
1959	420.8	2.02	58	28.7
1958	374.9	1.84	43	23.4
1957	347.2	1.68	26	15.5
1956	295.5	1.36	21	15.4
1955	234.5	0.89	15	16.9
1954	203.1	0.70	11	15.7
1953	188.3	0.57	8	14.0

It should be noted that the preceding figures are somewhat exaggerated because P/E multiples of most stocks were expanding during this period, but not quite to this extent. (See Appendix "B"). Between 1953 and 1961, American Home's stock advanced 875%. Without *any* multiple expansion, the advance would have been "only" 278%.

But a stock's P/E ratio is more than just a relationship of the current price to annual earnings. It is a thermometer of investor attitudes toward a particular stock within the context of its environment. These attitudes encompass future earnings growth and the certainty of those earnings. Further, one can, and should, compare this thermometer reading to the price earnings ratio of the overall market. Either the Dow Jones Industrial Average (Appendix "B") or Standard & Poor's are commonly used as comparative indices. The "market" price earnings ratio reflects the sum of all investors' attitudes on the future, including the outlook for the economy, as well as returns on competing investments. And the market will generally pay more when alternative investments are less attractive. For this reason, investors watch the level of interest rates. When interest rates are high, P/E multiples tend to be low and vice versa. The ratio also varies among industries, and even within a single industry. Usually, more will be paid for a dollar of earnings in a bull market than in a bear market (sometimes enthusiasm feeds upon itself). Further, more will be paid for a dollar of rising earnings than for declining earnings.

"The stock market looks cheap!" How often have you heard this comment? In this instance, the "market" is the Dow Jones Industrial Average. "Cheap" refers to what you have to pay to buy current earnings. But how cheap is cheap? Consider the wide swing in the Dow Average; 7 times earnings in 1949 to 23 times in 1961. Was 7 cheap? Not necessarily. Actually the Dow in this century has sold as low as 3.8 times earnings in 1917 (in this case, based on the mean price for each year) and as high as 38 times earnings in 1933. The year 1933 was in the depths of the depression. Why was the P/E so high? Because the price earnings multiple anticipated better times ahead when earnings were at or near their lowest point. In 1933, the market was close to its lowest level. On the same basis, then, the lowest multiples of earnings are sometimes recorded when investors regard those earnings as peak earnings. They're saying that earnings may not be going higher and they don't want to pay much for peak earnings.

Twenty years ago, the P/E multiple of the Dow Industrials was near 20 times earnings which tells us that investors were quite optimistic about the future. . . certainly more so than they have been in recent years.

Sometimes price earnings multiples don't matter. Most "asset plays" such as oil and gas exploration companies or mining companies, frequently sell at extremely high price/earnings multiples despite often erratic earnings records. These companies tend to be valued on the basis of reserves in the ground and "cash flow" (earnings plus all non-cash expenses such as depreciation and depletion) rather than earnings.

However, for most industrial stocks, analysts tend to compare a company's earnings and dividend prospects with that of the overall market to determine whether it is undervalued.

Further, the P/E of the target stock can be compared to other stocks in its industry. For example, if Digital Equipment were selling at 18 times earnings, IBM at 12 times earnings, and the Dow Industrials at 9, then Digital is being valued at 50% more than IBM and twice the "market." This is a quantitative evaluation of investor views about earnings growth rates.

In the early 1970's, most money managers were eagerly buying growth stocks. The idea was that persistent earnings growth of 10 to 15% was worth a high multiple and that there was less risk in buying a growth stock selling at 35 times earnings and risking a decline to 25 times than buying a cyclical stock at 12 times peak earnings that could eventually go to six times depressed earnings. As it turned out, this thesis was irresistible to the big banks (particularly those in New York City) and money managers were buying proven growth stocks like Avon, IBM, Xerox, etc. . . . Eventually, the list of "provens" was narrowed down to about fifty stocks, the so-called "nifty fifty." "Growth" they said, "would never go out of style." Buying for growth meant that these money managers could avoid income stocks, or acquisition candidates or cyclical turnarounds. All they had to do was concentrate on the big growth companies and pour tens of millions of dollars into the market. What they didn't realize was that, while growth would not go out of style, you could pay too much for growth. The inevitable result: when earnings faltered, stock prices crashed!

Now the reverse is true. Excessive Government spending, inflation, and high interest rates have taken their toll on P/E multiples since the 1960's. While it has been a difficult investment environment in recent years, it could also be a major benefit to buyers of super stocks in the years immediately ahead.

The Score Card

Ultimately, the real mark of a super stock is a strong and persistent demand for the company's products and services. The Super Stock Score Card is not a predictive device, but rather a reliable screen of nine specific categories that have been reviewed carefully. This screen merely tells us that the company is well-positioned to meet that demand and to return a good profit to the stockholders. Each of these categories was found common to most super stocks of the past. Collectively, they are only a starting point for further analysis. The long term picture and the company's fundamentals need to be examined with care. And, more times than not, an investor can anticipate a company's success by plain 'ole common sense.

Of these categories listed, seven are assigned "points." A score of 80 points or more tells us this investment has the characteristics of a future super stock. Less than 80 suggests that the company be reviewed again later, or that the stock be dropped altogether.

Thus far, all of these categories have been described in some detail. Now, let's construct the score card for your future stock selections...

- SIZE: There are no points assigned to this category. However, a company with sales between $25 million and $500 million should be given priority.

- UNIT SALES VOLUME (Max. 15 Points): Assign 15 points to the score card if, over the past three years, sales increased by a greater amount (total percent) than did CPI in the same period. See Appendix "A." If applicable, adjust prior years for acquisitions. For each year CPI outpaced sales growth within the past three years, deduct 5 points.

- PRETAX PROFIT MARGIN (Max. 15 Points):   A rising trend in pretax margins over the past five to ten years is awarded 10 points. Add 5 points if the pretax margin currently is above 10%. Deduct 3 points for each year (within the past three years) that the pretax margin declined from the preceding year.

- RETURN ON STOCKHOLDERS' EQUITY (Max. 30 Points):   In your judgment, does the company (within the next two years) have the potential for an annual return of at least 15% on average stockholders' equity? If the answer to this question is "no," rate this category "zero points" and proceed to another investment opportunity. If so, add 25 points to the score card. Add another 5 points if ROE is *currently* above 15%. Deduct 10 points if ROE is not in a rising trend (over the past five or ten years), taking into account the possibility that recent figures may have been unduly depressed by an economic recession.

- RELATIVE EARNINGS PER SHARE GROWTH (Max. 20 Points):   If, over the past three years, the company's earnings per share advanced by a larger percentage increase than that calculated for per-share earnings of the Dow Industrials, add 20 points. Any adjustments or allowances for extraordinary events that may have disrupted the company's normal performance during this period should be made with care. Many companies report "non-recurring" problems regularly.

- DIVIDENDS (Max. 5 Points):   No points are awarded
  to a company that does not pay a dividend or
  if the dividend trend over the past five years
  is not rising. If the dividend is in a rising trend
  and the payout ratio is below 40%, add 5 points.
  If the payout ratio is above 40%, the 5 points
  are not awarded *unless* the Earned Growth
  Rate is above 7.5%.

- DEBT STRUCTURE (Max. 10 Points):   If the company's long term debt is below 35% of
  stockholders' equity, add 10 points. Add only
  5 points if long term debt is above 35% (but
  less than 50%) of stockholders' equity. Do not
  award any points if long term debt is more than
  50% of stockholders' equity. If debt exceeds
  stockholders' equity, *deduct* 10 points.

- INSTITUTIONAL HOLDINGS (Max. 5 Points): Assign
  5 points to the score card if institutions do not
  own more than 10% of the outstanding shares.
  If more than 10% (but less than 15%) is held,
  add only 2 points. Do not award any points if
  institutional ownership exceeds 15% of the
  outstanding shares.

- PRICE EARNINGS MULTIPLE: While there are no
  points assigned to this category, super stocks
  will, by definition, outperform the overall
  market over the long term. It is not unusual
  for a super stock to temporarily underperform
  other stocks in a bear market. However, if the
  stock has not been advancing at least as well
  as the Dow Jones Industrial Average in a
  favorable market environment, beware! This
  factor can be a useful confirmation of your
  analytical work.

The Search Begins

Introduction

Financial practice without the emotional experience of investing has been regarded by cynics as impractical. One answer to the cynics is to point to the success of major graduate business schools such as Harvard, Stanford, and Columbia who train managers for industry through "practice." In other words, by analyzing and solving actual business cases, in time, the student's skills are polished to a high degree without the pain or expense of industry apprenticeship. Similarly, we can profit by analyzing some actual "cases" — statistical profiles of companies to fine tune our ability to uncover a super stock. As these cases demonstrate, in the real world, some judgment is needed. Unfortunately, stock selection is still an art as much as it is a science.

Case I: Alpha Corporation

Our first case study is a company we'll call Alpha Corporation, in the initial stages of marketing a new product that seemed to be a technological marvel of sophistication and great utility.

It's the first quarter of 1960. By leafing through the over-the-counter stock reports or reading the Wall Street Journal, one would have been impressed by the 1959 earnings report of Alpha: Sales up 15%; earnings per share up more than 22%. A quick look at the stock's price record indicated that it had gradually been advancing. Finally, another good sign, a 4 for 1 stock split had been effected in December, 1959. Further investigation is definitely warranted.

Financial references such as *Standard & Poor's, Moody's* or *Barron's* would have provided the sales and earnings record over the past nine years as follows:

	Total Revenues	Net Income Per Share
1959	$31,739	$.60
1958	27,576	.49
1957	25,807	.46
1956	23,560	.40
1955	21,390	.38
1954	17,318	.27
1953	15,751	.20
1952	14,755	.19
1951	12,897	.16

Alpha's record over the years has fulfilled initial expectations. Seeing statistics of this type make the drudgery of financial investigation worthwhile.

Knowing that a new product or process can create substantial increases in earnings, the serious searcher may have sifted through an average of a dozen companies each month that initially appeared to have interesting possibilities. A brief investigation of the past five (or ten) year record would usually show a start-and-stumble sales and earnings record. . .up and then down, or flat, for several years, then up again. Erratic operating figures would probably be our first reason for elimination of a stock from our list. In this case, Alpha's growth has been not just steady, but accelerating. Alpha's 1958 performance was especially impressive when compared to other companies at that time.

Size, too, is a common rejection factor. Many companies with sales over a half billion dollars, particularly in the late 1950's, would be culled from the list. This is not to say that large, older companies cannot grow, too. Occasionally, they do. In fact, during this time frame of 1950 to 1960, one old-line large company did do well: DuPont. DuPont was *the* chemical producer and from 1953 to 1955 it's earnings and future prospects looked extremely attractive. An investment in DuPont in 1953 tripled by 1955. But that was unusual. During this same period most of the big chemicals, steels, aluminums and auto manufacturers were poor investments. However, Alpha's record is different and the company's size in terms of sales is about right. The growth trend is strong: sales up 146% and earnings per share up 275%. That's the type of fast track growth we want. But will further research disappoint us? You be the judge. The statistics that were available back in early 1960 are presented on the next page.

As noted earlier, the company's current sales rate (in 1959) suggests the proper size range: large enough to grow and finance itself, but not so large that it has the built-in drag of large numbers.

A review of a more detailed financial statement such as Alpha's annual report or a Standard & Poor's or Moody's analysis sheet indicates that sales during the 1950's have been rising faster than the current rate of inflation (as measured by the Consumer Price Index). Also, see Appendix "A." In the ten years covered, not only have dollar sales gone up, but unit sales volume has also increased. Further, it is worth noting that sales have included a small but growing portion of equipment rentals and royalties which are more stable revenues.

The pretax profit margins can be calculated from the data by dividing the pretax income by sales as follows:

	Sales, etc.	Pretax Income	Pretax Profit Margins
1959	$31,739	$4,681	14.7%
1958	27,576	3,734	13.5
1957	25,807	3,399	13.2
1956	23,560	2,936	12.5
1955	21,390	2,642	12.4
1954	17,318	2,079	12.0
1953	15,751	1,685	10.7
1952	14,755	1,509	10.2
1951	12,897	1,088	8.4
1950	10,027	1,048	10.5

The tabulation is eloquent enough: Alpha's margins are in a rising trend. Note the steady increase over the years and the strong showing in 1958, a recession year.

ALPHA CORPORATION SELECTED FINANCIAL DATA
(Thousands of Dollars)

	1959	1958	1957	1956	1955	1954	1953	1952	1951	1950
Sales/Gross Revenues	$31,739	$27,576	$25,807	$23,560	$21,390	$17,318	$15,751	$14,755	$12,897	$10,027
Pre-tax Income	4,681	3,734	3,399	2,936	2,642	2,079	1,685	1,509	1,088	1,048
Income Tax	2,600	2,107	1,905	1,634	1,480	1,195	1,135	1,009	687	548
Net Income	2,081	1,627	1,494	1,302	1,162	884	550	500	401	500
Dividends (Common)	793	658	645	637	450	400	370	321	302	299
Long Term Debt	4,800	2,900	3,000	3,002	3,008	3,013	768	873	977	—
Stockholders' Equity	17,615	14,715	12,600	11,056	7,959	7,246	6,773	6,593	5,096	4,873
Common Shares Outstanding (Thousands)	3,460	3,309	3,265	3,225	3,085	3,085	2,265	2,265	2,265	2,265
Per Share ($)										
Net Income	.60	.49	.46	.40	.38	.27	.20	.19	.16	.20
Dividends	.21¼	.20	.20	.20	.14½	.13	.12	.12	.12	.12

Of all the measurements we are likely to use, the *return on stockholders' equity* calculation is the most important. Stockholders' equity is the total of the common stock account and retained earnings (net earnings less dividends). Another way to calculate stockholders' equity would be to deduct total liabilities from total assets — what's left, belongs to the stockholders and can be defined as stockholders' equity. The return on stockholders' equity is computed by dividing the net earnings by the stockholders' equity figure. For example, the return on equity for the year 1959 was 11.8% developed as follows:

$$\frac{\text{Net Income (1959)}}{\text{Stockholders' Equity (1959)}} = \frac{\$2,081}{17,615} = 11.8\%$$

These figures are not entirely accurate, however, because we are using total company income earned during the entire year, but only a year-end equity figure. It would be more accurate to use an *average* equity figure, obtained by averaging the year-beginning and the year-ending stockholders' equity totals. However, we're mostly interested in the long term *trend* and *potential.* In this regard, the companies we definitely want to avoid are those that could *never*, even under optimistic circumstances, enjoy a return on equity of 15% or more. For this screening purpose, year-end figures are satisfactory. But once we examine the company more closely, we want to be more precise:

	Net Income	Average Stockholders' Equity	Average Return on Equity
1959	$2,081	$16,165	12.9%
1958	1,627	13,658	11.9%
1957	1,494	11,828	12.6%
1956	1,302	9,508	13.7%
1955	1,162	7,609	15.3%
1954	884	7,010	12.6%
1953	550	6,683	8.2%
1952	500	5,845	8.6%
1951	401	4,985	8.0%

Again, the test is passed with flying colors. During the decade of the 1950's, Alpha increased average stockholders' equity to more than three times what it was in 1951. At the same time, net income advanced to five times! Some judgment is involved, however. Investors in 1958 may have wondered, for example, whether a "new trend" had set in after three years of declining returns. But in long term perspective, Alpha's return on equity was well maintained in the recession year 1958 when compared with the early 1950's. In addition, investors also knew by this time that a 15% return was not out of the question.

A return of 10-12% on equity during the decade of the 50's was well above average; not only for Alpha's business but also compared with the overall return on equity in American industry. To determine what constitutes an above-average rate of return, we must compare the company's return against those of its competitors and against overall corporate results during the period measured.

How did Alpha's per share earnings growth compare to the per share earnings growth of other stocks over the past few years? Here is a fast way to see:

	Alpha's EPS	Dow Industrial Average EPS*
1959	$0.60	$34.31
1956	0.40	33.34
% Change	+ 50%	+ 3%

*see Appendix "B"

In other words, by comparing the most recent earnings with the earnings of three years earlier, it is obvious that Alpha's progress has occurred *despite* the environment.

The dividend criterion is relatively easy to develop. Essentially, we want a company whose dividend policy is one of sharing some of its annually generated cash profits with the owners (shareholders). However, with a company that's effectively managed and positioned in a growing business, there are always innumerable profit opportunities that require money. Accordingly, as long as these opportunities exist, the company should be retaining its profits to invest for more profits. This means a low dividend payout as a percentage of net income.

In Alpha's case, the percentage is developed by dividing net income into annual dividends to determine the payout percentage as follows:

	Net Income	Dividends	Percent Payout
1959	$2,081	$793	38.1%
1958	1,627	658	40.4%
1957	1,494	645	43.2%
1956	1,302	637	48.9%
1955	1,162	450	38.7%
1954	884	400	45.2%
1953	550	370	67.3%
1952	500	321	64.2%
1951	401	302	75.3%
1950	500	299	59.8%
	+316%	+165%	

The resulting figures are somewhat surprising for a growth stock. The dividend payout was initially high — 60% to 75% of earnings for several years before gradually falling back to below a 40% payout. We would prefer less payout and more plowback, as is usually the case with fast growing companies. Nevertheless, the payout is not too high and dividends are rising. Overall, dividends paid increased each year in the ten year period. This important factor will attract both individual and institutional investors.

The test for a moderate to low debt structure depends, not so much on total debt, but on the relationship of debt to the company's financial structure. Of greatest concern would be long term debt as it relates to the capital structure. In most companies, short term debt is more than offset by current assets: cash and equivalents, account receivables and inventories. Within the production cycle, short term debt is usually incurred to finance inventories of material needed to produce the product or service. After these inventories go through the production process and result in products or services that are shipped or billed, they become accounts receivable. Thus, while our current debt remains the same, inventories have been reduced and accounts receivable increased. After a 30 to 40 day billing cycle, the accounts receivables are paid off by the company's customers. The cash is used to pay off or reduce the current debt. Our focus, as an investor, is on long term debt since this is not self-liquidating, but depends on profits over time.

Long term debt is usually expressed as a percent of total assets. But this measurement is too broad. Total assets include current as well as fixed assets and may be misleading since the type and quality of assets are not quantified. One other measure is more to the point: long term debt as a percent of stockholders' equity. Less than 35% is comfortable. Above 100% (1 to 1) is considered high when the return on equity is less than 20-25%. In this case, the percentages develop as follows:

	Long Term Debt as % of Stockholders' Equity
1959	27.2%
1958	19.7%
1957	23.8%
1956	27.2%
1955	37.8%
1954	41.6%
1953	11.3%
1952	13.2%
1951	19.2%

Our next test of a super stock is the level of institutional holdings. How many institutions were interested in Alpha Corporation in 1960? Not many. As a matter of fact, except for one university and a few local banks, there was only minimal interest. All to the good. A few astute investing groups have discovered what we did, but not many. That leaves room for a substantial price move once large institutions become interested. Institutional holdings are listed in Standard & Poor's and in Vickers.

There is no better gauge of increasing investor enthusiasm for the company than a rising trend in the price they are willing to pay for a dollar of earnings; that is, the price earnings multiple. First consider the years 1950 through 1953. They were war years — the Korean Conflict. Investor attitudes were affected by the tug of two psychological factors: a widening of the war and wage/price controls. Accordingly, multiples meant little until after the Armistice in the summer of 1953. This was succeeded by a slowdown of the national economy from the summer of 1953 through 1954. It is more relevant, then, to measure investor attitudes in terms of multiples for 1955 through 1959, a normal four years of a peacetime economy.

	Earnings Per Share	Price Per Share High/Low	Price Earnings Ratio High/Low
1959	$ .60	$36 1/2 - 21 1/4	60.8 - 35.4
1958	.49	24 1/4 - 11 7/8	49.5 - 24.2
1957	.46	15 3/8 - 9	33.4 - 19.6
1956	.40	18 3/8 - 11	45.9 - 27.5
1955	.38	16 3/4 - 7 3/4	44.1 - 20.4

Here we see a gently rising price earnings ratio — nothing spectacular — but an indication that the investing community is paying increasing attention to the company's operating performance. Is the price earnings ratio too high? We don't know. The Dow Jones Industrial Average was selling at about 20 times lacklustre earnings in early 1960. So, with Alpha's stock at $32, the multiple accorded these growing earnings did not seem out of line.

The trend of a rising P/E multiple cannot, of course, continue forever. Stocks do go down from time to time. For this reason, we are concerned with Alpha's performance both compared with *itself* and compared with the *market* as a whole. We note that Alpha's average P/E increased from 32.3 in 1955 to 48.1 in 1959. In the same period, the Dow multiple increased from 12.3 to 18.3 times. Both advanced about 49%. However, Alpha's earnings were *up* while the earnings of the Dow Average *declined*! This not only speaks favorably for Alpha's fundamentals, but for its investment merit as well. It simply would have been more profitable to own Alpha than to own the Dow Industrials in this period.

In summary, let's review our analysis:

- Size: Nearly $32 million in sales — a small but growing company. The right size.

- Unit Sales Volume: Rising; up 28.4% over CPI since 1956 without a "negative" year. (15 points)

- Pretax Profit Margins: Above 10%; upward trend, rising every year over the past 8 years. Full point score. (15 points)

- Return on Stockholders' Equity: Above-average returns and rising. Capable of achieving at least 15%. (25 points)

- Relative Earnings Per Share Growth: Substantially better than the DJIA over the past three years (+ 50% vs DJIA + 3%). (20 points)

- Dividends: A rising dividend trend and a current payout ratio that will allow for a plowback of earnings. (5 points)

- Debt Structure: Long term debt is not too high in relation to stockholders' equity. In 1959, debt was 27% of stockholders' equity. (10 points)

- Institutional Holdings: Low. (5 points)

- Price Earnings Ratio: Upward trend in line with the market.

According to our criteria, Alpha Corporation, with a total of 95 points, has all the ingredients of a super stock. But can we be sure? Should we wait and see evidence of a more vigorous earnings trend? The more we wait for verification, the higher the price we'll have to pay. But let's say we wanted to be sure and we waited another year. Now it's early 1961. . .and the trend continues but at an increased pace with sales of $37 million up 17% over 1959, net income of $2,598,329, up 25% over the prior year, and the stock price is approaching $100 per share, a triple in the price.

In real life, Alpha Corporation is actually Haloid Xerox, now called Xerox Corporation. Although it was incorporated more than 50 years earlier, it did not break into super stock status until 1959 or 1960. The company, in 1959, was about to introduce its new Model 914, which marked the beginning of a revolution in office copiers. But you didn't have to know this — at least not initially — to recognize the stock's potential. In reality in 1960, however, without knowing that Haloid Xerox equipment being shipped was RENTED and not SOLD, an investor looking only at the numbers could have been temporarily misled. The earnings benefits (and the return on equity) for the equipment being shipped to the field were not realized immediately. Actually, the company's return on equity declined in 1960 and did not being its sharp ascent until 1961 (17.1% that year): 33.4% in 1962; 34.3% in 1963; and 36.4% in 1964! For this reason, it is important to judge a company's performance, not just on a year-to-year basis, but with a longer term perspective.

The rest, of course, is stock market history. By 1965, sales had multiplied more than tenfold, in only five years, to an incredible $392 million! Net income was $58.6 million! By the end of the 1960's, sales passed the billion dollar mark! Here are some of the appreciation percentages:

- For the very patient, the rewards were — as Dr. Samuel Johnson once said — beyond the dreams of avarice. A purchase of 100 shares of Haloid Xerox in 1958 for $4,750 — a year before our discovery became 6,000 shares in 1972 worth $1,031,250!
- In one year — 1963 — you could have bought Xerox in the first week of the year at a price of $150 to $160. In the last week of the year sold it for $435, an increase of 180% in twelve months! In the next eight years, the stock more than quintupled again!

Indeed, there were many plumbers, taxi drivers and housewives in Rochester, New York who were too lazy (or too smart) to sell their Xerox stock. They are now (and have been for a while) millionaires!

These results are eloquent testimony to the rewards of finding a super stock!

Case 2: Beta Corporation

Our second case study, called Beta Corporation, may or may not be a super stock. It is for you to decide. Presented is a brief description of the company and its operations and selected array of statistics. A worksheet has also been provided for you to use in calculating the company's qualifications.

Beta Corporation's business can be characterized as a growth area relying heavily on innovative products that appeal to the consumer. Basically, the business can be called entertainment and its growth and profitability depends on consumer disposable income.

The time frame has been moved forward several years to 1966. This was a period of the Great Society of President Lyndon Johnson and one of two wars; one on poverty and another in Vietnam. Inflation was low (but beginning to climb) and high-grade, long term bonds were being sold at the then unbelievably high interest rate of 6%.

Our constant review of the financial section of newspapers gives us an idea of significant corporate operating results both quarterly and annually. One day we come across the results of the Beta Corporation for the latest September fiscal year as follows:

"Beta Corporation announced net profits after taxes for the fiscal year (52 weeks) ended October 2, 1965 of $11,378,778, representing $6.08 per share on the 1,870,097 shares outstanding at the fiscal year end. This compares with last year's (53 weeks) net profit of $7,057,435 equal to $3.83 per share on the 1,837,942 shares then outstanding. . .gross revenues reached a record high totaling $109,947,068, an increase of $23,295,960. . ."

Beta Corporation is reporting astounding fiscal results. Gross revenues increased more than 26% but net income increased more than 61%. Beta Corporation is well worth further investigation. But come to your own conclusion. In this case study, and in the others that follow, you will be given a ten year summary of all the statistics needed to make the necessary calculations. Follow the same line of reasoning used in the Haloid Xerox example and fill out the "score card."

BETA CORPORATION SELECTED FINANCIAL DATA
(Thousands of Dollars)

	1965	1964	1963	1962	1961	1960	1959	1958	1957	1956
Sales/Gross Revenues	$109,947	$86,651	$81,922	$75,612	$70,248	$50,931	$58,432	$48,577	$35,778	$27,565
Pre-tax Income	21,529	12,749	12,674	10,914	9,788	(2,642)	7,300	7,790	7,499	4,464
Income Tax	10,150	5,692	6,100	5,650	5,322	(1,300)	3,900	3,925	3,850	1,841
Net Income	11,379	7,057	6,574	5,264	4,466	(1,342)	3,400	3,865	3,649	2,623
Dividends (Common)	738	707	685	665	650	648	608	615	299	—
Long Term Debt	8,851	9,451	11,798	15,505	15,360	20,397	6,266	6,591	2,373	593
Stockholders' Equity	53,125	41,494	34,998	29,024	24,425	20,610	24,398	22,205	18,982	16,359
Common Shares Outstanding (Thousands)	1,870	1,838	1,833	1,830	1,830	1,830	1,833	1,890	1,890	1,654
Per Share ($)										
Net Income	6.08	3.83	3.59	2.88	2.44	(.73)	1.86	2.04	1.93	1.59
Dividends	0.39	0.38	0.37	0.36	0.36	0.36	0.33	0.33	0.16	—

   Additional facts that were not in the financials, but could
have been researched, are given as follows:
   Institutional holdings: According to a 1966 Standard &
Poor's *Stock Guide*, 17 institutions hold 134,000 shares, or
about 7% of the 1.9 million total shares outstanding.
   Almost from the outset in 1966, Beta's stock price as well
as most other stocks, seemed to be in a steady decline.
However, Beta was clearly outperforming the market. At the
end of April, 1966, the stock was still well above its lows of
the fourth quarter of 1965; the Dow Industrials had fallen much
further.

| | Beta P/E Ratio | | Dow Industrials P/E | |
	High	Low	High	Low
Early 1966	Approximately 9.6x		Approximately 17.0x	
1965	10.3	6.4	18.1	15.7
1964	12.9	9.6	19.2	16.5
1963	12.2	7.2	18.6	15.7

BETA CORPORATION
SUPER STOCK SCORE CARD

                                                      Score

- Size*..................................... (Confirm)

- Unit Sales Volume........................

- Pretax Profit Margins....................

- Return on Stockholders' Equity............

- Relative Earnings Per Share Growth.......

- Dividends................................

- Debt Structure............................

- Institutional Holdings....................

- Price Earnings Ratio*.................... (Confirm)
                                          Total _____

*No score necessary

Conclusion:

With the calculations and score card completed, let's analyze the results.

Beta has nearly $110 million in sales, more than three times the sales size of Haloid Xerox when it first appeared in our financial readings. Larger, indeed, but well within our range of interest.

Sales volume has been in a significant uptrend over the ten year period. Again, while it's difficult to equate dollar volume with unit volume, our basic standard is that sales volume increases should not be solely the result of price increases due to inflation. Checking the Counsumer Price Index in Appendix "A" would verify that the year-to-year sales increase, especially in the past three years, were well ahead of the year-to-year increases in the CPI. Sales advanced from $75,612,000 in 1962 to nearly $110,000,000 in 1965, an increase of 45% while the CPI in the same period rose only about 5%.

Pretax profit margins (net income before taxes, divided by sales or, in this case, gross revenues) are healthy and have been rising — another plus for super stock status. However, we note that 1960 was unprofitable and that margins declined in 1964.

Management's efficiency in generating an attractive return on the stockholders' investment is also well demonstrated in this ten year period. Return on stockholders' equity (net income after taxes divided by stockholders' equity) has been in an uptrend and well above 15%. However, one year — 1960 — deserves further investigation. When related to the rate of return earned on stockholders' equity for other corporations during the comparable period, this company's return is especially noteworthy. In 1965, the Earned Growth Rate was more than 25%!

In the past three years, Beta's earnings advanced from $2.98 to $6.08 per share, an increase of 111%. This growth compares to a 47% increase for the Dow Jones Industrials. . .from $36.43 in 1962 to $53.67 in 1965. This is certainly a positive sign.

Cash dividends have been in an uptrend since they were first paid in 1957. Further, the percent payout is modest to allow a large percentage of earnings to be plowed back into corporate expansion.

The level of the debt structure in the corporation appears to be reasonable. Measured against stockholders' equity, the percentage of long term debt is low. Note, too, that we do not necessarily need a ten year record of debt levels. The most recent years are particularly relevant. In this case, the favorable comparison of the past two years is valid.

Institutional holdings are small.

Summarizing Beta's Super Stock Score Card:

	Score
• Size – Satisfactory	—
• Unit Sales Volume - rising each year and well above inflation; up 40.7% over CPI since 1962.	15
• Pretax Profit Margins - above 10% and rising; deduct 3 points for 1964.	12
• Return of Stockholders' Equity - above 15% and rising.	30
• Relative Earnings Per Share Growth - favorable (+111% vs DJIA +47%)	20
• Dividends - rising slightly with low percentage payout.	5
• Debt Structure - low, 17% of stockholders' equity.	10
• Institutional Holdings - low.	5
• Price Earnings Ratio - mixed. Could be rising relative to the market, but inconclusive.	—
Total Score	97

This looks like a super stock.

In real life, Beta Corporation is Walt Disney Productions, a stock that enjoyed superior performance twice in two decades. The first time was in the early 1950's when the stock moved from a low of 8 5/8 in 1954 to a high of 48 3/4 in 1957. That year the stock moved from over-the-counter trading to a listing on the New York Stock Exchange and the stock continued its advance. In 1954, the Company was still small. Total revenues were only $11.6 million with net profits of $733,852. Total shares outstanding were 652,840.

During 1957, stockbroker reports were estimating sales above $35 million for the year and a net profit increase of more than 30%. Actually, they were right on sales and wrong on profits — net profits were up 39%. The new theme park opening in 1955 in California was becoming more important.

Disney would have qualified for super stock status in 1957, but investors would have been buying into an unsustainable momentum. The subsequent years of 1958 and 1959 witnessed a slowdown in sales and earnings growth and, in 1960, the company showed a loss as well as a decline in sales.

What happened is instructive for future stock selection. Haloid Xerox spoiled many investors; its fast growth continued in full vigor, unabated for more than a decade. However, growth trends do not continue indefinitely. Developing a trend line from past statistics and projecting that trend endlessly into the future is an exercise in arithmetic futility. It just doesn't happen that way. There are rarely constant, uninterrupted long term earnings trends; only episodic bursts of growth, a pause, and then another spurt of growth. In 1957, Disney was nearing the end of one period of growth. Sales and earnings would continue in an uptrend for two more years, but at a much slower rate. The year 1960 was a year of transition from one growth period to another, which proved to be even greater. The 1960 Disney Annual Report indicates that the loss that year was caused by a write-down of inventories and a decline in film revenue and television income. The decline in television income was due to the fact the the "Zorro" and "Mickey Mouse" shows were not televised in 1960. Finally, publications, music, records and other merchandising revenue also declined. The two pieces of good news: Disneyland Park revenues increased and the Company bought out the 34.5% stock interest in Disneyland held by ABC-Paramount for $7,500,000 in cash and notes. This buyout made Disneyland, Inc. a wholly-owned subsidiary.

Ahead, in the late 1960's and early 1970's, would be *Mary Poppins*, continued increases in profitability at Disneyland and, of course, the big profit potential which was in the early planning stages in 1965: Disney World in Florida.

The 1966-67 period proved temporarily uneventful for Disney's earnings, although the stock price continued to move ahead, largely in anticipation of Disney World. Earnings growth resumed in 1968 and, by 1973, a $1,000 investment made in 1966 would have been worth more than $17,000.

Walt Disney puts to rest the claim by some growth stock proponents that you should invest only in technology. One difficulty in technology investing is determining which of today's leaders will also be the technical leaders of tomorrow. Skilled analysts have been known to make wrong judgments on the future. And even if they're right on the technology, they may be wrong on management's ability to carry the technology forward to a profitable conclusion. Witness the famous example of Sperry Rand versus IBM in the early days of computer development. In the 1950's, experts would have argued that Sperry's Univac Computer was far ahead of anything IBM had or could develop in the near future. But IBM had superb marketing management — enough to give them a winning position early in the game. In the case of Haloid Xerox, we let the statistical record lead us to a conclusion. It was more efficient in time and money, and more effective than analyzing the qualitative aspects of the products.

In the case of Walt Disney, the company and its record had to be analyzed more closely despite the fact that the products, films, books, and theme parks can all be understood by the average investor. Whether we like Snow White or Disneyland has little meaning in terms of Disney's investment qualities. Stripped of emotion, of warm affection for their likeable products, Disney emerged as a super stock candidate strictly based on our score card characteristics.

Case 3: Gamma Corporation

Our third super stock exercise concerns a company in a relatively prosaic sector of the packaging business. The time is early 1975. When reviewing the fourth quarter and year-end results for 1974 you are struck by the annual report of our third case study: Gamma Corporation. In a recession year with poor earnings results the norm, Gamma has reported 1974 earnings of $2.20 per share. This is up more than 21% over the 1973 results of $1.81 per share. Gamma's record is one of the few significant sales and earnings increases you have seen in several weeks of reviewing numerous 1974 operating results. However, total sales in 1974 exceeded our $500 million size limit. But Gamma is only the fourth largest manufacturer in its field with less than 10% of its industry revenues. The record suggest that this company is definitely worth investigating for super stock possibilities.

The analysis of the financial record reaffirms our suspicions. This is the earnings per share record for the past ten years:

Year	Earnings per Share
1974	$2.20
1973	1.81
1972	1.58
1971	1.41
1970	1.26
1969	1.11
1968	1.01
1967	.91
1966	.80
1965	.71

Earnings increased each year for the last ten years. Even beyond that, an inspection of the record back into the 1950's indicated no evidence of a "down year." Moreover, Gamma weathered the recession of 1967 and 1970 nicely. A remarkable performance. A study of the annual reports and other financial data sources reveal the following information for the analysis:

- Standard & Poor's or other authorative sources indicated institutional holdings for Gamma as follows: 26 institutions owned a total of 1.4 million shares (8% of the outstanding stock).
- Further research shows that price earnings ratios, while declining, have been gradually improving relative to the market:

	Gamma P/E Ratio		Dow Industrials P/E	
	High	*Low*	*High*	*Low*
1974	9.6x	6.2x	9.0x	5.8x
1973	15.8	10.6	12.2	9.1
1972	17.4	11.7	15.4	13.2
1971	16.6	12.3	17.3	14.5

GAMMA CORPORATION
SUPER STOCK SCORE CARD

Score

- Size .... (Confirm)
- Unit Sales Volume ....
- Pretax Profit Margins ....
- Return on Stockholders' Equity ....
- Relative Earnings Per Share Growth ....
- Dividends..................................
- Debt Structure ....
- Institutional Holdings ....
- Price Earnings Ratio..................... (Confirm)

Total _____

Conclusion:

GAMMA CORPORATION SELECTED FINANCIAL DATA
(Thousands of Dollars)

	1974	1973	1972	1971	1970	1969	1968	1967	1966
Sales/Gross Revenues	$766,158	$571,762	$448,880	$448,446	$414,161	$370,903	$337,118	$301,147	$279,830
Pre-tax Income	72,961	61,013	56,093	53,034	52,628	47,805	42,291	33,366	29,429
Income Tax	33,298	26,725	24,900	24,560	26,770	24,800	21,389	14,529	12,880
Net Income	39,663	34,288	31,193	28,474	25,858	23,005	20,902	18,837	16,749
Dividends (Common)									
Long Term Debt	34,413	37,922	31,234	41,680	37,490	36,271	40,871	56,131	57,890
Stockholders' Equity	262,650	243,916	230,366	211,847	193,508	172,937	150,105	129,567	110,841
Common Shares Outstanding									
(Thousands)	18,001	18,894	19,727	20,212	20,408	20,659	20,641	20,634	20,607
Per Share ($)									
Net Income	2.20	1.81	1.58	1.41	1.26	1.11	1.00	.91	.80
Dividends	—	—	—	—	—	—	—	—	—

GAMMA CORPORATION

SUPER STOCK SCORE CARD CRITIQUE

	Score
• Size - big in terms of sales, but acceptable related to the industry.	—
• Unit Sales Volume - rising trend and above inflation, except in 1972. Deduct 5 points.	10
• Pretax Profit Margins - below 10% and not in a favorable trend, even considering the recession.	0
• Return on Stockholders' Equity - a somewhat favorable trend, but watch out! What will happen to the sales and earnings growth rates if management ever decides to pay a dividend? A 15% ROE is not enough!	30
• Relative Earnings Per Share Growth - unfavorable (+ 56% vs. DJIA + 80%).	0
• Dividends - none. Definite negative for a company at this stage. It is easier to be forgiving with new or younger companies.	0
• Debt Structure - low; a positive rating.	10
• Institutional Holdings - acceptable.	5
• Price Earnings Ratio - declining, but performing better than the market.	—
Total	55

Conclusion: Gamma Corporation is a growth stock, but not a super stock. Size is a negative, but not fatal. Pretax profitability is a question. Normally, the lack of a dividend is not critical for a new company. But this is not a new company. However, management's stated policy of not paying a dividend is a major drawback. Moreover, a closer look at the figures reveals only a 12.0% average compounded growth rate in pretax income over the past eight years — despite plowing every penny back into the company! Finally, as explained in Chapter III, any company with a 100% plowback can grow internally no faster than its return on equity will allow — in this case, 14-15% per year. This is *without* any dividend. What will happen if they decide, as they should, to pay one?

Gamma Corporation was not deemed to be a super stock and its stock price performance proved to be satisfactory, but unspectacular, in the years following this study. Actually, the company is Crown Cork and Seal, a major factor in the container industry where it has positioned itself in fast-growing markets. Crown Cork is a good example of excellent financial growth, but not quite making it in the super stock category.

Case 4: Delta Corporation

The fourth case study represents the genesis of a basically one-product company. The time: March, 1968. By reading the financial section of the morning paper you notice the 1967 results of our example, Delta Corporation. Sales are reported at $36.9 million, up 16.0% over 1966, and net income increased 3.4% to $3,714,000. Not too bad for a recession period.

Though not spectacular, what catches your eye is the comment about the last half of 1967 — sales up 35% and earnings up 20% from the year-earlier period. It is not a bad idea to read more than the first paragraph of a news release. Further, you read that Delta's 1967 sales were nearly *ten times* greater than the company's sales ten years ago, and that net earnings were more than *thirty times* larger than earnings in 1957. Delta seems to be just the right size with superior operating results. Could Delta be a super stock?

In addition to the financial data, additional information on price earnings ratios and institutional holdings could be found from traditional sources:

	Delta P/E Ratio		Dow Industrials P/E	
	High	*Low*	*High*	*Low*
1967	22.4x	9.4x	17.5x	14.6x
1966	15.4	7.6	17.3	12.9
1965	16.4	10.1	18.1	15.7
1964	15.3	11.6	19.2	16.5

Standard & Poor's Monthly Stock Handbook showed that 8 institutions owned 266,000 shares, or 10.5%.

DELTA CORPORATION SELECTED FINANCIAL DATA
(Thousands of Dollars)

	1967	1966	1965	1964	1963	1962	1961	1960	1959	1958
Net Sales	$36,928	$31,010	$24,056	$18,184	$14,370	$10,804	$6,824	$6,417	$5,550	$3,975
Pre-tax Income	7,079	6,790	6,021	5,109	3,817	2,836	1,575	968	713	213
Income Tax	3,365	3,203	2,846	2,582	2,002	1,442	806	492	360	94
Net Income	3,714	3,587	3,175	2,527	1,815	1,394	769	476	353	119
Dividends (Common)	621	569	500	402	327	148	110	73	55	44
Long Term Debt	3,300	—	—	—	—	—	—	53	143	58
Stockholders' Equity	17,773	14,677	11,653	8,965	6,552	5,042	3,768	3,109	2,706	2,400
Common Shares Outstanding (Thousands)	2,524	2,517	2,510	2,498	2,250	2,230	2,202	2,202	2,202	2,202
Per Share ($)										
Net Income	1.47	1.43	1.27	1.01	.81	.62	.34	.21	.16	.05
Dividends	.25	.23	.20	.16	.15	.07	.05	.03	.03	.02

DELTA CORPORATION
SUPER STOCK SCORE CARD

Score

- Size .... (Confirm)
- Unit Sales Volume.........................
- Pretax Profit Margins ....
- Return on Stockholders' Equity ....
- Relative Earnings Per Share Growth ....
- Dividends.................................
- Debt Structure ....
- Institutional Holdings ....
- Price Earnings Ratio...................... (Confirm)

Total _____

Conclusion:

DELTA CORPORATION

SUPER STOCK SCORE CARD CRITIQUE

	Score
• Size - approaching $50 million — a good size.	—
• Unit Sales Volume - rising significantly faster than inflation. Double check for acquisitions.	15
• Pretax Profit Margins - well above 10% and rising longer term. A poor trend in 1965-1967 period (deduct 9 points), but now showing definite signs of rising.	6
• Return on Stockholders' Equity - still well above 15% and rising. Compared to prior recession (1960, 1958) years, 1967 showed substantial progress and very recent figures suggest improvement ahead.	30
• Relative Earnings Per Share Growth - favorable (+46% vs. DJIA +16%).	20
• Dividends - small payout, trend is up.	5
• Debt Structure - low position	10
• Institutional Holdings - low and acceptable, but not as low as we'd like.	2
• Price Earnings Ratios - rising.	—
Total	88

Conclusion: A possible super stock. Or, at the very least, this stock deserves further analysis. Good growth rates in both sales and earnings seem likely to continue. Delta Corporation appears to be performing well in a poor environment. Furthermore, the company's operations are, even now, quite profitable and could be getting better.

Our hypothetical Delta Corporation is in actuality Masco Corporation, a major producer of single-handle faucets, the "Delta" faucets with a patented mechanism. In 1967, more than 20 million faucets of all kinds were sold, of which, 25% were single-handled faucets and Masco was the leading producer of this product.

The obvious question to be asked at this point is: Will the market for faucets of this type be saturated any time soon? And what is the company's ability to develop or acquire new products? You notice by reading the annual report that Masco acquired another business in 1967. In the report, management states that this acquisition is one significant reason for the decline in pretax margins and ROE in the most recent year. Now, it appears, Masco's profitability could be even better than the figures suggested at first glance.

How well did this investment fare? Five years later, in 1972, Masco reported earnings of $14.4 million on sales of $134 million. Earlier that year, the stock reached a price of $65½, up 400% from the adjusted March, 1968 price of $13. Today, Masco has sales approaching $1 billion and in recent years, the stock has been above $40 per share after another 2 for 1 stock split in 1975.

Case 5: Epsilon Corporation

The time is May, 1970 and for one entire evening you've been looking through a book of stock charts for new ideas. Almost every stock is down. As an initial filter, you decide to consider only those stocks that: (1) Have declined by about 50% or more from prices of 3-6 months earlier; (2) Are under $500 million in sales; (3) Are showing increases in earnings in both the past year and in the most recent quarter; (4) Have little or no long term debt; and (5) Have pretax profit margins of at least 15%.

In the search, it hasn't been difficult to find stocks that have declined 50%. However, finding companies that are showing any earnings increases, let alone 15% margins, is becoming quite a bit more of a challenge! Most of the drug companies seem to show earnings gains, but then few are down 50% in price. Many of the technology companies are down 50%, but so are their earnings. The desire for little or no debt is due to concern over the recent trend of sharply higher interest rates. However, one that passed the filter is a company we'll call Epsilon Corporation. Total 1969 revenues are reported at $434,503,000 up a modest 4% from the $418,620,000 reported in 1968. Net income of $4.00 per share was up 13% over the 1968 net of $3.55 per share, adjusted for the 3 for 2 stock split in May, 1969. The report also says that 1969 set a new record for Epsilon, both in revenues and earnings. In addition, the first quarter in 1970 also showed gains.

A quick check of the company's record indicates that the company is positioned in an attractive segment of a major natural resource industry. Revenues increased more than 32% from $318.1 million in 1965 to $420.6 million in 1969. And earnings per share went up even more rapidly, from $2.34 per share in 1965 to $4.00 in 1969, a 71% increase.

But what about size? Last year's sales were more than $420 million. That would seem to indicate Epsilon could already be too large to show significant increases in sales and earnings in future years. We would prefer a smaller company, but remember "large" and "small" are not absolutes; they are relative standards. Size depends on the company in its industry context. A $400 million sales company in a business serving a multi-billion-dollar market would not be considered big. And a review of Epsilon Corporation indicates that it is basically a service company supplying essential needs to huge companies positioned in the resource extraction business.

Beyond size, the question is: Does this company match our requirements for a super stock? If we assume that only five years of key reference data are available, is it possible to make an evaluation? The operating and stock data are presented here in summary form.

EPSILON CORPORATION
SELECTED FINANCIAL DATA

(Millions of Dollars)

	1969	1968	1967	1966	1965
Net Sales/Revenue	$420.6	$409.1	$369.2	$343.1	$318.1
Pre-tax Income	74.8	68.3	52.0	49.3	47.7
Income Tax	28.5	27.3	20.5	21.1	20.6
Net Income	46.3	41.0	31.5	28.1	27.1
Dividends (Common)	16.0	11.6	9.2	8.9	7.7
Long Term Debt	—	—	8.9	11.8	12.4
Stockholders' Equity	344.3	321.3	293.6	266.8	252.6
Common Shares Outstanding	11,565	11,600	11,543	11,394	11,540
Per Share ($)					
Net Income	4.00	3.55	2.75	2.45	2.34
Dividends	1.28	0.95	0.80	0.78	0.67

In addition, here is information not contained in the five-year summary:

1.   The rate of return on stockholders' equity for all corporations in the U.S. was 11.9% in 1969. In Epsilon's particular industry it was 14.2%.

2. A check of institutional holdings indicates that in 1969 fifteen institutions held 488,000 shares or 4.2% of the stock.
3. The Company's price earnings ratio record was as follows.

	Epsilon P/E Ratio		Dow Industrials P/E	
	High	*Low*	*High*	*Low*
1969	27.5x	19.1x	17.0x	13.5x
1968	25.8	13.0	17.0	14.3
1967	18.2	9.8	17.5	14.6
1966	16.4	10.7	17.3	12.9
1965	15.6	12.5	18.1	15.7

Now you are ready to analyze the operating record of Epsilon and see how it rates on the Super Stock Score Card.

EPSILON CORPORATION
SUPER STOCK SCORE CARD

Score

- Size . . . . (Confirm)

- Unit Sales Volume . . . .

- Pretax Profit Margins . . . .

- Return on Stockholders' Equity . . . .

- Relative Earnings Per Share Growth . . . .

- Dividends . . . .

- Debt Structure . . . .

- Institutional Holdings . . . .

- Price Earnings Ratio . . . . (Confirm)

Total _____

Conclusion:

EPSILON CORPORATION

SUPER STOCK SCORE CARD CRITIQUE

	Score
• Size - big in terms of sales figures, but not too large relative to its industry.	—
• Sales Volume - rising above CPI each year, except for 1969. Overall, sales rose 8.8% above the inflation rate (1966-69).	10
• Pretax Profit Margins - above 10%; rising, without any major decline. Deduct 3 points for 1967.	12
• Return on Stockholders' Equity - rising and 15% does not appear impossible.	25
• Relative Earnings Per Share Growth - favorable (+ 63% vs. DJIA – 1%).	20
• Dividends - rising dividends with a low payout ratio.	5
• Debt Structure - not significant in 1970.	10
• Institutional Holdings - favorable	5
• Price Earnings Ratio - a rising trend, improving vs. the market.	—
Total	87

Conclusion: Epsilon Corporation is a possible super stock. The company is engaged in a promising business and any meaningful sales growth following this difficult economic period could lead to substantial earnings improvement and a sharply higher stock price.

In this example, Epsilon Corporation is, in actual corporate life, Schlumberger, Ltd., a technically-oriented company supplying wireline services to the petroleum industry including geological services, contract drilling and other oil well services. The company also manufactures electronic equipment and instrument control systems.

Had Schlumberger been identified in the early months of the 1970 decade, through 1975, the company would have fulfilled our wildest expectations. Total operating revenues from sales and services in 1975 were $1.6 billion, compared to $421 million in 1969, while net income increased to $219.3 million compared to $46.3 million in 1969. More to the point, adjusted for two splits during the period, earnings per share increased from 89 cents to $3.92 and the stock price rose from under $12 to nearly $100. This performance is impressive considering the period 1970 thru 1975 encompassed one really bad stock market experience in 1973-74.

However, there was no particular reason to sell Schlumberger at the end of 1975. All of the super stock indicators were still intact — rising sales, increasing margins, return on equity, and so on. The three growing negatives were its size, an increasing debt and the widening institutional participation. Still, by late 1980, the stock reached as high as $130 (after three more splits) compared with the adjusted prices of $30 in 1975 and a low in 1970 of under $4.

Case 6: Bristol-Myers Company

William McLaren Bristol   *John Ripley Myers*

Without using a fictitious name, let's look at Bristol-Myers Company as our final case study. The business was founded in 1887 by William M. Bristol and John R. Myers with an initial investment of $5,000. After 70 years, the company reached $100 million in sales and, 14 years after that, $1 billion. But within that 14-year span, actually from 1957-67, Bristol-Myers was indeed a super stock. Over this 11-year period, the stock price advanced an average of 31% per year — not including the added benefit of dividends. That Magic Combination was in full force! But first, let's go back in time.

It's early 1957. BMY shares are about $45 on the New York Stock Exchange. The earnings report for 1956, which has just been released, indicates profits of $3.54 per share, up 19% from the $2.97 per share of 1955. At the current price, the stock is valued at about 11 times estimated 1957 earnings, while the dividend yield is a little better than 4%. The company has a modest amount of debt, the pretax margin is a respectable 12%, and the return on stockholders' equity appears to be approaching 15%. Not bad!

BRISTOL-MYERS COMPANY

Portrait of a Super Stock 1957 to 1967

Year	Sales ($mm)	Pretax Margin %	Net Income ($000)	Return On Avg. Equity %	Per Share Earn.	Per Share Div.	Payout Ratio %	LT Debt % of Equity	Average Stock Price $	Average P/E Ratio
1952	$ 56.6	8.9%	$ 2,589	7.6%	$0.13	$0.14	108%	39%	2 1/2	20.0x
1953	55.5	9.1%	2,541	6.9%	0.12	0.08	69%	38%	1 7/8	15.4
1954	62.4	11.6%	3,604	9.5%	0.18	0.08	46%	35%	2 1/4	12.8
1955	75.7	12.1%	4,866	12.4%	0.25	0.13	51%	33%	2 5/8	10.5
1956	89.4	12.2%	5,586	14.0%	0.30	0.15	49%	29%	3 1/8	10.3
1957	106.8	13.3%	6,404	15.3%	0.34	0.17	49%	25%	4 1/2	12.5
1958	113.9	12.0%	7,235	15.3%	0.37	0.18	49%	21%	5 1/2	14.9
1959	131.5	14.1%	8,889	15.6%	0.43	0.22	50%	16%	8 7/8	20.6
1960	146.7	15.7%	10,768	16.3%	0.52	0.26	51%	13%	13 1/8	25.2
1961	164.4	16.9%	12,957	17.9%	0.62	0.30	49%	10%	21	33.9
1962	198.8	17.3%	16,094	20.0%	0.77	0.38	49%	8%	20 1/8	26.1
1963	232.4	17.9%	19,132	21.2%	0.91	0.45	49%	5%	26 3/8	29.0
1964	265.0	18.1%	23,095	22.7%	1.09	0.53	49%	4%	32 3/8	29.7
1965	391.4	16.6%	33,357	26.6%	1.32	0.65	49%	—	41 3/4	31.6
1966	468.5	17.1%	39,402	26.2%	1.57	0.75	48%	—	50 1/8	31.5
1967	730.1	13.7%	52,019	25.0%	1.86	0.95	51%	30%	67 7/8	36.5
1968	827.0	13.9%	57,120	20.7%	1.96	1.10	56%	27%	71 3/8	36.4
1969	928.2	14.2%	67,606	21.5%	2.23	1.20	54%	23%	64 1/2	28.9
1970	981.2	14.5%	74,112	20.8%	2.41	1.20	50%	43%	61 3/8	25.5
1971	1,066.4	13.2%	75,767	18.9%	2.44	1.20	49%	38%	63 1/8	25.9
1972	1,201.2	12.6%	83,935	18.5%	2.60	1.20	46%	27%	64 5/8	24.8
Growth Rate*	21.2%		23.3%		18.8%	18.8%			31.2%	

Note: Stock Splits. . .3 for 1 in 1959; 2 for 1 in 1963; 2 for 1 in 1966   *Average 1957-67.

A closer look at the company's financial statements reveals that cash and marketable securities, nearly $15 million, comfortably exceeds total current liabilities of $9 million, while the current ratio (total current assets divided by total current liabilities) is better than 3 to 1... another healthy sign. It is also interesting to note that Bristol-Myers' advertising, selling and administrative expenses represent the largest cost item on the income statement. These are, for the most part, variable costs that can be managed. Moreover, the cost of sales figure, only about one-third of sales, has been rising less rapidly than sales. In short, the company's profitability appears good and could be getting better if the products sell.

Bristol-Myers' sales in 1956 were classified into three or four major categories, the most important being Toiletries & Cosmetics (39%), Proprietary Medicines (32%), and Prescription Medicines (18%). Research expenditures, about $3.2 million that year, seemed to be divided between the Products Division, which is now enjoying success with its new *Ban* roll-on deodorant, and the Bristol Laboratories Division, which has just recently introduced *Tetrex*, an improved tetracycline antibiotic. Clearly, more new products seem likely. In addition, it appears that management is interested in expanding the product line further through acquisitions.

Would it have been possible for an investor in 1957 to know that Bristol-Myers could be another super stock? What do you think?

Now, with three decades of 20/20 hindsight, can we in the 1980's expect to profit from the lessons and the case studies cited here? Yes, with a little work! And Finding The Next Super Stock will make that effort worthwhile!

Be An Analyst

Complete, reliable and up-to-date information about companies and industries is fundamental to identifying super stocks. Your decisions are only as good as your information. Good investment information is of three types:

(1) Timely and general information about business, the stock and bond markets, and individual companies. Sources include newspapers and magazines. The object is to keep in touch with trends and to develop a list of possibilities that can be screened down to a few more promising prospects for further research as potential super stocks.

(2) Specific information about interesting industries and companies. Much of this material can be found in your public library, your stockbroker's research department and financial and investment advisory services. For specific corporate information, there is also the company itself. At this point in your research, you have screened dozens of possibilities down to a few prospects. Detailed information, sufficient to develop your super stock score card, is then obtained from company sources. Most companies will place you on their mailing list for financial material, including annual reports (the last five years if possible), the most recent quarterly reports, news releases, and reprints of articles and speeches by management. The latter may be useful as perspective since managements usually cover a great deal of operating history when they speak before analyst groups throughout the country.

A letter addressed to the Secretary of your target company requesting information is often all you need. The company address can be located in the Business Section of your local library. For example, most libraries carry the Standard & Poor's Directory which lists company officers and addresses.

(3)   The Securities & Exchange Commission Reports. Under law, nearly all companies whose stocks are traded publicly must file certain documents with the SEC. These reports are extensive. The most important are the 8K, 10K, and 10Q reports. For basic analysis purposes, only the 10K is needed (this is a detailed report on company operations required and filed with the SEC).

The first and most important part of the 10K includes a business description, five-year summary of operations, listing of properties and parent corporations and/or subsidiaries, legal proceedings and financial statements. The second part relates to management, its pay and benefits and the principal security holders. Sometimes 10K reports are available from the reporting company. If not, then a copy can be obtained from the SEC for a fee by writing to:

The Securities & Exchange Commission
Washington, D.C. 20025

Timely and general information begins with a daily reading of the *Wall Street Journal*. This is literally the Daily Bible of current investment information and will keep you current on corporate and economic news. *Barron's*, a weekly, is less topical and more detailed than the *Journal*. There are always a handful of in-depth articles on financial, corporate or economic subjects directed to investors. Separate sections cover the weekly events in the stock market, bond markets, commodities, options and foreign investment. Also included are several research pieces on interesting stocks. Finally, *Barron's* is packed with weekly stock and bond tables, indicators and other financial data. This weekly is a "must" for the serious investor.

Business Week magazine, also a weekly, covers a broader business beat: not only economic and finance, but also marketing and labor events. Corporate problems and successes are given extensive coverage and they usually stimulate some investment ideas.

Forbes is published bimonthly with a focus on the average investor. Companies, industries and individuals are portrayed in a readable and stimulating manner.

Finally, the *Wall Street Transcript* is a weekly with unusual coverage. Each issue publishes dozens of brokerage reports on companies as well as industries. It also includes a number of top management speeches at security analyst society meetings during the prior week. All in all, the *Transcript* is a lengthy compendium of investment material that was previously published. Its point of view is that of the professional on Wall Street. It serves as compiler of more information than you will need or have time for; not to mention sometimes being out of date. But it's nice to have it in your home library and once in awhile, leafing through it, you will get a worthwhile idea.

Specific information about companies and industries can be found by visiting your library. There, you will find the output of three major investment advisory services: Moody's, Standard & Poor's and Value Line. Moody's Manuals are a basic source of historical data, bound in large and complete volumes published annually for most Industrial, Utility, Transportation and Finance companies.

Standard & Poor's publishes a series called *Standard Stock Reports* covering those stocks listed on the New York Stock Exchange, American and the Over-the Counter markets. Each stock is summarized on a single sheet which includes a description of the company, a chart of the company's performance and detailed statistical data. Standard & Poor's also publishes a smaller and useful *Stock Guide*; literally a handbook issued monthly with one-line summaries of more than 5,000 common and preferred stocks.

Value Line produces a service that summarizes (again, on one sheet) individual company statisitics and prospects. More than 1,500 companies are covered. The service is available at most libraries or through:

Value Line Investment Survey
Arnold Bernhard & Company, Inc.
711 Third Avenue
New York, NY 10017

Also, much of this specific information can be found at your local brokerage office. As a matter of fact, stock brokerage firms are a superb source of company and industry information. The larger firms, such as Merrill Lynch and Bache, maintain platoons of stock analysts who produce volumes of information, all of it free to clients.

Since you need a stockbroker to transact orders anyway, it makes sense to select a broker who can provide the information you need on companies as well.

SEC Reports may be obtained from either the Commission or sometimes directly from the company. The most important reports are the 8K, the 10K and the 10Q. However, for basic analysis, only the 10K is really needed. The 10K is a detailed report on company operations, usually much more specific than the annual report. If requested, 10K reports are frequently available from the reporting company. If not, then a copy may be obtained from the SEC. (Also see page 138).

Recommended Books

Investors looking for the next super stock can discover a terrific selection of books at the local library. If the library doesn't have the book you need, *ask* for it! Most libraries can obtain volumes from wholesalers on very short notice. Learn to use R. R. Bowker's *Books in Print* and the *Books in Print* supplements. The key is simply to know *what* you are looking for. The community library can be an investor's best friend.

Each year publishers unleash a flood of "how to" books on investments. Many of these are of the "get-rich-quick" variety and, like diet books that sell on the basis of instant reader satisfaction, so do finance books sell on becoming rich overnight. Few books can be considered authoritative and worth shelf space in your home. Only a half dozen have passed the test of time; that can be read and re-read and still convey a sense of learning each time. The six are:

(1) ***The Intelligent Investor*** by Benjamin Graham (1973), published by Harper & Row.
This book, a classic of its kind, touches the principles of sound investing by advocating a point of view with which some may not agree. Nonetheless, it still contains rich insights. The late Ben Graham was one of the most respected investment authorities of the past fifty years.

(2) ***The Battle for Investment Survival*** by Gerald M. Loeb (1957), published by Simon & Schuster.
Gerry Loeb was a successful stock broker who made millions practicing what he preached; to wit: let the stock market guide your investments. One of his basic tenets was never, ever average down on a stock... but do average up. Most investors do the reverse. Gerry was fond of saying that in the 40's and 50's making money in Wall Street was a "battle" and by the 1970's (before he died) it was a war.

(3) ***Understanding Wall Street*** by Jeffrey B. Little and Lucien Rhodes (1978), published by Liberty Publishing Company.
This invaluable, easy-to-read guide explains the basics of investing, as well as many of the principles on which this book is based. Written by two experienced analysts, *Understanding Wall Street* is comprehensive and fully illustrated. Updated at each printing.

(4) ***How to Make Money in Wall Street*** by Louis Rukeyser (1974) published by Doubleday.
A witty and useful overview of how the stock market works and what makes its practioners, the analysts, stockbrokers and portfolio managers, tick. Rukeyser's

decades of reporting on the financial scene, including hosting the television program "Wall Street Week," has produced a perspective that is both informative and engaging for all investors.

(5) *Investment Analysis and Portfolio Management* by Cohen, Zinbarg and Zeikel (1967), published by Richard D. Irwin. An authoritative college textbook on the investment process. It is detailed and somewhat tedious but close to the last word on the subject and, through recent editions, up-to-date.

(6) *Understanding the Economy — For People Who Can't Stand Economics* by Alfred L. Malabre, Jr. (1975), published by Dodd, Mead and Company.
A primer on how our economy works by a *Wall Street Journal* staffer.

While this basic reading list is modest, it forms a core reference library; something to which you can refer time and time again over the years. Extensive reading beyond these books may be enjoyable but less productive in terms of time and effort. Your available reading time is better spent in reviewing periodicals in the search for stock ideas.

Economic Background

From time to time it is useful to determine where you might be in the business cycle and the future economic trend. Forecasting requires a searching out of indicators that might tell the future shape of the economy. Remember, it is the trend that is important. Your figures should encompass at least two key weekly indicators that telegraph when a trend is about to change. For example, look at paperboard production and railroad carloadings. The rationale for paperboard as a leading indicator is that nearly all products are packaged or wrapped. So, a change in production could signal a boom or a slump. The second is railroad carloadings, which is a summary of cars being loaded for shipment each week. Since everything produced must be shipped, and a lot is shipped by railroads, a change here could be most significant.

Economic details to know:

- *GNP* - Gross National Product is the total of all goods and services produced in the U.S. on an annual basis. This is reported by quarters.
- *Employment and Unemployment Figures* - figures are issued on a monthly basis.
- *Disposable Personal Income* - how much money people have to spend.
- *Consumer Debt* - too much debt is a caution signal.
- *Cost of Living Index* - the inflation rate at the consumer level.
- *Interest Rates* - the Prime Rate and Long-term Bond Rates should be watched. Pay attention to both the level and direction of rates. Most Wall Street observers wish they could forecast rates, especially by watching the varied signals of Federal Reserve policy. Unfortunately, there is little predictive value in any of the interest rate indicators.
- *Commodity Prices* - price changes in sugar, wheat, copper, and so on, often signal price changes in the industries they affect. Gold is unique as a barometer of investor confidence worldwide. So, usually, a downward trend here means good news for investors, an uptrend indicates future problems. Finally, the dollar is a fairly good indicator and sometimes spells trouble for major U.S. exporters, such as agriculture.

If you're going to read and develop a feel for the economic environment, you'll be running into terms that have peculiar meanings. Dictionary definitions won't quite do. Here are eight economic terms, simplified, to help you on your way:

- *Business Cycle*: The sequence of expansion and contraction of economies. The cycles vary from one year to a decade. Usually recessions have lasted 18 months to two years. Also watched are fifty-year cycles.
- *Trough*: The bottom of an ordinary, short-term cycle. Usually, at this point, coincident indicators such as Gross National Product and Industrial Production stop falling.

• *Recovery*: The phase when business begins to improve — sales and employment figures go up.

• *Recession*: A contraction of business. Usually identified as two quarters of negative Gross National Product (no growth).

• *Depression*: Usually the word means a deep, severe recession. However, economists seem to disagree on a workable definition which illustrates the difficulty of quantifying economic concepts. For example, the term "Depression" is usually in quotes with "Great" sometimes added. More appropriately, several economists have used numerical levels to distinguish a depression from a recession: over 10% unemployment is a minimum, while the more useable figures appears to be 15%. In the 1930's unemployment hit an estimated 25% of the work force.

• *Inflation*: When price levels are rising and the dollar shrinks in value and buys fewer goods.

• *Deflation*: When price levels are falling and the dollar gains in value and has greater buying power.

• *Disinflation*: A slowing of the rate of inflation.

ROE for Selected Industries in 1981

	Return on Equity %		Return on Equity %
Aerospace	15.9%	Office Equipment	15.2%
Airlines	Nil	Oil Service, Supply	24.8
Appliances	10.8	Paper, Forest Products	11.0
Automotive	Nil	Personal Care Products	17.7
Banks	13.6	Publishing, Broadcasting	17.2
Beverages	15.4	Railroads	12.5
Building Materials	7.0	Real Estate, Housing	7.1
Chemicals	13.1	Retailing (Food)	15.1
Conglomerates	15.4	Retailing (Nonfood)	12.5
Containers	10.7	Special Machinery	12.5
Drugs	18.7	Steel	9.4
Electrical, Electronics	15.9	Textiles, Apparel	11.4
Food Processing	14.9	Tire & Rubber	9.2
Food & Lodging	17.1	Tobacco	19.9
Instruments	12.7	Trucking	13.9
Metals & Mining	9.0	Utilities	13.0
Natural Resources	18.6		
		All Industries	14.0

Appendix A

**Thirty Five Years of
Inflation Trends
Consumer Price Index
Annual Changes in Percent
( ) Denotes Decrease**

1984	*4.5* *4.2*		
1983E	+ 5.0 *3.2*	1965	+ 1.9
1982E	+ 6.5 *6.1*	1964	+ 1.2
1981	+ 8.9 *10.4*	1963	+ 1.6
1980	+ 12.4 *13.5*	1962	+ 1.2
1979	+ 13.2	1961	+ 0.7
1978	+ 9.0	1960	+ 1.6
1977	+ 6.8	1959	+ 1.5
1976	+ 4.8	1958	+ 1.8
1975	+ 7.0	1957	+ 3.0
1974	+ 12.2	1956	+ 2.9
1973	+ 8.8	1955	+ 0.4
1972	+ 3.4	1954	(0.5)
1971	+ 3.4	1953	+ 0.6
1970	+ 5.5	1952	+ 0.9
1969	+ 6.1	1951	+ 5.9
1968	+ 4.7	1950	+ 5.8
1967	+ 3.0	1949	(1.8)
1966	+ 3.4	1948	+ 2.7

Red figures from U.S. Commerce Dept.

Sources: *Statistical Abstract of the U.S.* and *Economic Indicators* issued by the Joint Economic Committee, Author estimates.

Appendix B

Dow Jones Industrial Average
Earnings and P/E Ratios

	EPS	High P/E	Low P/E
1981	113.71	9.0	7.4
1980	121.86	8.2	6.2
1979	124.46	7.2	6.4
1978	112.79	8.0	6.6
1977	89.10	11.2	9.0
1976	96.72	10.5	8.9
1975	75.66	11.7	8.4
1974	99.04	9.0	5.8
1973	86.17	12.2	9.1
1972	67.11	15.4	13.2
1971	55.09	17.3	14.5
1970	51.02	16.5	12.4
1969	57.02	17.0	13.5
1968	57.89	17.0	14.3
1967	53.87	17.5	14.6
1966	57.68	17.3	12.9
1965	53.67	18.1	15.7
1964	46.43	19.2	16.5
1963	41.21	18.6	15.7
1962	36.43	19.9	14.7
1961	31.91	23.0	19.1
1960	32.21	21.3	17.6
1959	34.31	19.8	16.7
1958	27.95	20.9	15.6
1957	36.08	14.4	11.6
1956	33.34	15.6	13.9
1955	35.78	13.7	10.8
1954	28.18	14.4	9.9
1953	27.23	10.8	9.4
1952	24.78	11.8	10.3
1951	26.59	10.4	9.0
1950	30.70	7.7	6.4
1949	23.54	8.5	6.9
1948	23.07	8.4	7.2
1947	18.80	9.9	8.7
1946	13.63	15.6	12.0
1945	10.56	18.5	14.3
1944	10.07	15.1	13.3
1943	9.74	15.0	12.2
1942	9.22	13.0	10.1
1941	11.64	11.5	9.1

Index

Future Investment Opportunities

A book has its limitations in offering timely and specific advice. Consequently, a supplement to *Finding the Next Super Stock* is published regularly to help investors uncover new ideas for potential Super Stocks.

With the aid of a computer, and applying the criteria outlined earlier, the *Super Stock Source Book* identifies numerous Super Stock candidates from more than 3,000 companies under study.

A current edition of the *Super Stock Source Book* may be obtained by sending a check or money order for $4.95, plus $.50 postage, and your name and address to:

> Frank A. Cappiello
> c/o Liberty Publishing Company, Inc.
> 50 Scott Adam Road
> Cockeysville, Maryland 21030
>
> (Please make checks payable to Newport Counsel, Inc.)

Acknowledgements and Credits

All stock charts appearing throughout the text are reprinted courtesy of:

M.C. Horsey & Company, Inc.
120 South Blvd. Box H
Salisbury, Maryland 21801

The publisher thanks the following corporations for the use of their photographs and their assistance:

Page 8	Masco Corporation
Page 9	Tropicana Products, Inc.
	(Beatrice Foods Company)
Pages 10 & 11	Baker International Corporation
Page 12	Black & Decker Manufacturing Company
Pages 15 & 66	Texas Instruments, Inc.
Pages 53 to 57	Minnesota Mining & Manufacturing Company
Page 59	Xerox Corporation
Page 61	Walt Disney Productions
Pages 62 to 64	Johnson & Johnson
Page 134	Bristol-Myers Company